Life and Success: The Ultimate Blueprint

Your Companion In Your Quest To Be Successfull

S P Garg   **Neha Sharma**

© S P Garg and Neha Sharma 2022

All rights reserved

All rights reserved by authors. No part of this publication may be reproduced, stored in a retrieval system, or transmitted in any form or by any means, electronic, mechanical, photocopying, recording or otherwise, without the prior permission of the author.

Although every precaution has been taken to verify the accuracy of the information contained herein, the author and publisher assume no responsibility for any errors or omissions. No liability is assumed for damages that may result from the use of information contained within.

First Published in June 2022

ISBN: 978-93-5611-520-0

Price: INR 300

BLUEROSE PUBLISHERS
www.BlueRoseONE.com
info@bluerosepublishers.com
+91 8882 898 898

Cover Design:
Neha Sharma

Typographic Design:
Namrata Saini

Distributed by: Blue Rose, Amazon, Flipkart

Dedication

With the blessings of Lord Ganesha
Dedicated to the memory of my loving parents
Late Dr Surendra Prasad Garg
Smt. Leelawati Devi Garg

S P Garg

Dedicated

To my kids,

For inspiring me to transform my emotions into wisdom, my feelings into insight and my thoughts into words that paint the blank canvas of these pages.

Thank you,

and I love you

Neha Sharma

Preface

Life contains some exemplary embodiments, which not only teach us the methods to achieve what we aspire to, but also makes us understand the very crux of its attachments. This is a special book, not only for us but also for everyone who reads it. Life is easy yet intricate. It's beautiful in every way. And when we speak of success, it's not only a matter of having a good career, wealth, and power, but also of healthy relationships, inner peace, and love. True happiness can be found only when the meaning of true success is understood and for that, we need to peep inside our own self. Something that is success for one, might be inconsequential for other. So first and foremost, one needs to determine one's dreams and aspirations, and subsequently the roadmap towards success shall become evident. In this book, we have shared some of the most beautiful and inspiring life stories along with what we have learned from life so far. Life is a voyage which teaches us something substantial with each passing moment, and the process of enlightenment continue till the very last breath. This book is for everyone who's trying to find the real meaning of life, and how the expedition towards a successful existence can be fulfilled with ease. A wilful approach, a dedicated mind-set and a thorough understanding of oneself are the first steps to be taken, to reach one's goals.

And this book **"Life and Success: The Complete Blueprint"** will help the readers approach life with a broadened horizon.

We hope that this book appeals to you and helps you find answers to many questions surrounding you.

We would welcome your comments, review and suggestions.

Happy reading.

S P Garg
Neha Sharma
3rd March 2022

Contents

Part 1: Unravelling the meaning of life and success 1
   Chapter 1: The Meaning of Life 3
   Chapter 2: The Success and Failure Dichotomy 9
   Chapter 3: The Recipe of Success 13
   Chapter 4: Mental Health Is the Key 19
   Chapter 5: Embracing Your Failures 29
   Chapter 6: I Will Survive 35
   Chapter 7: Surrender (To) Your Dreams 49
   Chapter 8: Some Success Habits 53
   Chapter 9: Keep Away from Negatives in Life 61
   Chapter 10: Self-Expectancy 69
   Chapter 11: The personal success mantras to imbibe 73

Part 2: Success Blueprint 79
   Chapter 12: Ordinary People: Extraordinary Success 81
   Chapter 13: Success Blueprint for Entrepreneurs
   and Start Ups 119
   Chapter 14: Success Attributes for Leaders 139
   Chapter 15: Ultimately Life is for Happiness 153
   End Note: Keep On Walking 160
Acknowledgements 163
Author's Profile: Prof. S P Garg 166
Author's Profile: Neha Sharma 168

Part 1

Unravelling the meaning of life and success

Neha Sharma

"Sometimes, life can be mysterious and inexplicable and other times it can be easily accessed and deciphered as if everything in front of our eyes is like an open book.

While walking down the path towards our goals, we encounter various obstacles. These can be tricky enough to give us nightmares on some occasions and simple enough to be tackled easily on others.

The first step in understanding success is understanding life.

And once we are able to deduce what our life path is, the haze surrounding our chosen success dissipates in the blink of an eye."

Chapter 1

The Meaning of Life

"Life isn't about finding yourself.
Life is about creating yourself."
-George Bernard Shaw

Let's talk about the literal meaning of life. We all know that any matter that shows some characteristics of birth, growth, responsiveness to cause and effect and the transformation of energy and reproduction, can be called life. It is a process that starts with the birth of an entity, continuing as it grows and prospers, till the moment it breathes its last. There are millions of species of life, right from single-cell organisms like the amoeba, to mammoth ones like the blue whale. Amongst this myriad of species, we Humans are at the top of the heap, being the most evolved and conscious of them all.

Could there be a deeper meaning behind our existence and of the simplest organism? It's worth pondering. Many humans of immense calibre have thought along these lines through the ages, but a comprehensive answer remains elusive. We are still trying to understand life and all that it encompasses, to recognize the systematic and the spiritual, the physical, and the nonphysical.

Suppose someone is a little interested in the esoteric and hopes to rise above the mundane. In that case, it's only natural that this thought can plague our psyche quite frequently, especially when alone, with only our views for a company: the conception and end game of life itself. While pondering about the same, it's necessary to consider all its facets. Apart from the prominent aspect of our physicality, an analytical perspective should also be observed, given that we are not just a cluster of cells, embodying a distinct form, living for a certain period, and then departing.

To think about human beings and our society, we know that apart from intellectual capabilities, we also have an emotional quotient, the power of understanding, learning how to use and manage our own emotions in positive ways to relieve stress, having the capability to communicate effectively and overcoming challenges and most of the times, being aware of the steps required to defuse conflict.

We can think and reason, and these are traits that make us different from others who incorporate the lower strata of the organism table. Humans will be and thrive; the ability to conceive an idea and sets us apart from the more unevolved life forms. The others are just prisoners of their natural program and evolve unconsciously, locked in their genetic traits and habits.

To begin with, life seems like a puzzle, an unsolvable one, to be precise. We can never hope to decode it fully. Yet, to comprehend, realize, and acknowledge life's physical and scientific dimensions means nothing unless we also attempt to decipher it in its totality.

We commence our journey under a shadow of love, extended by our parents and our loved ones. Our first teachers are our parents, who contribute the most to the building blocks of our personality and value system. This is the foundation laid down by our parents, on which the whole structure of our disposition stands tall. We feel safe and secure with them, as their love and care are unblemished and unadulterated. It's love in the purest form. A mother feeding a new-born is the most unselfish act of all that is done willingly and with a sense of giving beyond the usual human tendency to look for payback for even the most minor favor.

Once out in the world, we start understanding life through the very glasses that our parents bestow upon us. This initial programming makes us capable as we strive to tackle life. Along the way, we contact others, in the influence of whom we willingly and unwillingly modify our approach, learning how to react and respond to our fellow human beings. As a result, we manage to imbibe positive and negative attributes. Likewise, we know how to be patient when facing difficulties, and sometimes impatience is all that we can contribute.

We learn how to be kind and compassionate in the real sense when seeing someone suffering, but sometimes greed and selfishness become prominent. We understand how to be competitive when facing opposition, but sometimes our doubts, fears, and insecurities steal the show. So, we learn a lot throughout this journey. And these learnings help us sail through the process of life.

To visualize life, imagine a roller coaster. An amalgamation of ups and downs, happiness, and sadness, smiles and tears, all rolled out on the same platform. You're forever buckled up, ready to sail through another round of blockbuster emotions. If you've ever been on a rollercoaster, you might be familiar with the butterflies that kick in when you're initially moving up the platform, a sort of nervous excitement akin to euphoria, thanks to a burst of adrenaline that runs through your entire body. When you're hurtling down, you might feel a sense of dread, a foreboding accompanied by a sinking feeling in your belly. Similarly, journeying through life, we feel satisfied and happy doing things we enjoy. However, when faced with less-than-ideal situations, our feelings become despair and pessimism, having no respite.

We feel as though nothing can be done to overcome life's complications; we imagine ourselves writhing in our misfortunes forever. But then, the only thing that helps us surface back is our patience and our dedication to triumph over all the problems that life has exposed us to.

The Meaning-of-Life Conundrum

The one thing that most people have in common is the belief that their lives are meaningless. They are constantly bemoaning their existence and questioning why they were sent down here in the first place. To be fair, it's a legitimate concern that might drive one crazy if pondered upon for a little too long.

So what is the purpose of our lives, and why are we here?

If we go through numerous philosophers' various conceptions and writings over the years, we will stumble upon varied answers. According to Aristotle, one of the greatest philosophers of all times, "Each man's life has a purpose and that the function of one's life is to attain that purpose." Herein he claims that the purpose of life is to find a purpose to live for, which in exchange might replenish you with happiness and contentment, which can be achieved by acquiring virtuous conduct and reason. His philosophy personified precedence of existence outlook that expresses that world knowledge begins by observing what exists. He taught that people could increase their understanding by increasing the evidence of the senses through reason.

So we can say that every human being has capabilities, and everyone should use their abilities to their fullest. This will help one achieve happiness and satisfaction in the real sense. Everyone has a purpose that gives you a specific framework to live your life to the fullest. What is yours?

Polishing Your Mind-set

Those who still feel that life has no meaning and are forever burdened by the sheer melancholy because of the thoughts of being purposeless need to refurbish our way of thinking to discover our true strength and self. A change of mindset is in order. We should not weigh self-worth only based on our professional success. We should contemplate other aspects like relationships, conduct with others, etc. Not everyone who's professionally successful is happy, and not everyone struggling at their workplace is unhappy.

The saying goes, the grass is always green on the other side. Everyone has different benchmarks and definitions of happiness and success. What is right for one might not be that good for another. We need to ascertain our own biases to live a life free from the shackles of societal thinking.

One more thing that helps us discover our strengths and weaknesses to work upon them is inspiration from others' life stories. The wise always strive to learn from others' mistakes. So many times, we stumble upon life tales of people that motivate us to the core. We feel that if these people could fight and win over all the odds in their lives, why can't we?

We are all unique and distinct in our ways. No two people are alike. Someone else's strengths can be our weaknesses and vice versa. The trick lies in exploring and discovering our strengths to put them to use and accept our shortcomings so that we can work upon them.

Chapter 2

The Success and Failure Dichotomy

"Success is the ability to go from one failure to another with no loss of enthusiasm."
-Winston Churchill

From the beginning of our lives, we are thrown headfirst into the never-ending race to be good and better and never stop until we're the best. Right from our early childhood, when the concept of success and failure are merely concepts, we are involuntarily forced to stand out for reasons beyond our comprehension. Whether being a competitive parent trying to live vicariously through their experiences or the peer pressure of trying to thrive and survive, the feelings of struggle and conflict are instilled within us for the rest of our lives.

Comparisons amongst children are a common issue created by the elders almost subconsciously. We're made aware of other people's achievements in a way that casts a shadow over our efforts in life. How then is a kid supposed to feel confident in his innate talents and abilities when he's constantly struggling with an inferiority complex that has stemmed from factors beyond his control?

And once you grow up, this process becomes even more stringent. Whether it's school or other activities, sometimes even simple breathing becomes a fight to prove that you're good enough. Our guardians compel us to go out of our ways, work and grind, and hustle till we reach simple goals that we probably didn't even set for ourselves. The intention behind such practices can be out of love for the kid or worry about his future, but the outcome is almost always negative. This mission towards triumph can leave them feeling drained, crestfallen, and alienated, sometimes even after immense success throughout the years.

However brilliant in arts, a child is not approved of if their performance in school is average. Their passion for something challenging for people around him to understand is disregarded and even frowned upon. Why do we forget that success cannot be confined to a few streams?

We need to accept that every child is different and has different capabilities. For example, a brilliant child in music might become a celebrated virtuoso only if supported from the very initial stages of life. And if the same child is forced to study science to become a doctor, he might fail miserably.

So, to understand success and failure, we must start from the very foundation of the concept. After recognizing one's strengths and limitations, one needs a stage to flourish. It could be a literal stage, a courtroom, or even behind a computer. Someone might be fascinated by planets and galaxies, whereas another child the same age might not be interested at all.

It's crucial to find out the choices, interests, and likings of kids and help them work on the same. For example, if a child is not interested in Maths and science, they should not be compelled to take up the subjects mentioned earlier. Instead, the child should be motivated to discover what they like doing the most.

That way, parents will be able to support them chose a career they can excel in.

If we analyse our society closely, we'll find that barring a few, most of the people around us are unhappy, no matter how much they have accomplished. Why is it so? If making money, having fancy cars, mansions, immense fame, and popularity was the prelude to a lifetime of happiness and success, then the ones at the top of their game wouldn't ever be miserable. But that is not always the case. One of the reasons behind this situation is working in a field that might not be their true calling.

So, understanding the concept of true success and failure is very important. We should always ask ourselves what entices us the most. That is something we wish to do. And even if we must choose a field that we are unsure of, give it your best shot, and keep working on your passion behind the scenes.

Even if you keep giving your passion some time and consideration, you will do much better in your regular work-life. For example, if you are very fond of music, and the stream chosen for further studies is engineering, don't give up on music. Allot some free time for it as well. It will not only make you feel energized and programmed for your chosen field but will also imbibe new enthusiasm and determination to do well in it.

Chapter 3

The Recipe of Success

"Take up one idea. Make that one idea your life–think of it, dream of it, live on that idea. Then, let the brain, muscles, nerves, every part of your body, be full of that idea, and just leave every other idea alone. This is the way to success."

"Awake arise and stop not till thy goal is reached"

-SwamiVivekananda

Our society has chalked up success into a fictitious weighing scale wherein we're all guilty of measuring our self-worth and self-esteem over how successful or otherwise one has become. This quest for success has become a never-ending rigmarole right from our school days when the rat race begins and then carries on in right earnest as childhood progresses to adulthood, middle age, and then onwards to old age.

This endless endeavor to be successful is fraught with many pitfalls that others in the rat race create for us out of their envy or mental derangement. Who doesn't wish to be successful? We all do; how else are we supposed to feel good about ourselves? The pressure to be successful is unconsciously applied to our psyche by our parents, peers, and rivals. To be first amongst equals has become the be-all and end-all of our existence. This perspective is the very thing that can hold us back from scaling the mountains of success.

Life and Success: The Ultimate Blueprint

Being successful should never be the reason why you finally decide to validate yourself ultimately; it's a personal perspective; what one considers to be the pinnacle of success may not be so in the eyes of others. Whether due to hard work or intelligence, validation of our achievements should be done naturally anyway, regardless of the circumstances. One must always look at success as something enjoyable, something exciting to achieve and experience, but it isn't the very foundation we build our life over.

Being objective about the circumstances is paramount because many things must click all at once to achieve our goals. Most of them are beyond our abilities to control; the best way is to ride the waves of fortune, rough or otherwise.

Keeping that in mind, what do you think are the ingredients to conjure up this delicious concoction called success? In the end, it's just a state of mind family success, business success, career success, etc., etc., are all about how others measure us against ourselves. Most of us consider ourselves successful if we do better than our immediate acquaintances paying little heed to the larger perspective of life itself. It is a blinkered vision of our existence or a narrow-minded evaluation of self-worth. Nonetheless, it's imperative that everyone who is part of the race sign up for it, so we might as well give it our best shot or roll over and die.

The proof of the pudding is in the eating, so everyone is always trying to find the secret ingredient that makes up super success; most of us would say that hard work is perhaps the main attraction of the entrée. And indeed, the path towards success is seldom forged upon a bed of roses without thorns or efforts without a little bit of sweat. But is it the only ingredient that matters? It's not invariably an indispensable ingredient to

Life and Success: The Ultimate Blueprint

personal and professional success, but even the best of gravy needs a little bit of *spice*.

We can't disagree with the fact that most of us are told that success can be achieved only if we grind till our backs give out from a very young age. Grinding is all well and good, but donkeys are the epitome of grinding. No one in their right mind condones a donkey's life, so hard work and grinding without intelligence is a fool's quest that leads to a merry-go-round situation wherein one feels they are moving very fast. Still, ultimately there is no headway, only going around in circles. And hence, senseless grinding on the journey to success leads to a life of utter hustle and hopelessness.

It helps to be hard working, of course, but can we say that only hard work leads to success. Unfortunately, the answer is a big NO. Hard work for the sake of hard work is not a very intelligent way of approaching whatever endeavor is to be undertaken. But, on the other hand, they successfully enjoy the journey because, along with hard work, they have mastered the art of seasoning the broth with essential condiments that make their success inevitable and sweet.

Here are some of the vital components that mark our way to success:

Intention

> *"When you find your WHY, you don't hit snooze no more!*
> *Instead, you find a way to make it happen."*
> *-Eric Thomas*

Intentions are what drive us towards the realization of our goals. If the intent is fuzzy, the end goal may never be achieved. Unless the choices are clear-cut, what can be the aspiration?

We can set our targets, and we can have a lot of clarity, but what we need to be sure about is the "why" behind its accomplishment. Haphazard and purposeless actions towards a set goal can often become the prime reason behind its sabotage, that is not to say that every step can be pre-planned because whatever may be the plan of action can be easily derailed by the imponderable or the inconceivable, as the saying goes there is many a slip between the cup and the lip. The best-laid plans of mice and men go awry. If we are not sure of the very purpose of the goal that we wish to achieve, we can become demotivated and let ourselves be distracted, leading to breaking away from our ambitions.

So before setting a goal, we must think about its alignment with our intentions and aims in life.

Zeal or passion

"There is no passion for being found playing small- in settling for a life that is less than the one you are capable of living."
-Nelson Mandela

The first and foremost step towards the path of success should be to discover our passion and pour our hearts into it; in other words, finding your mojo and not something that others have planned for you. Once you find it, your mission becomes quite clear, and so, you can set out to work towards its implementation with the requisite steps to be taken in the right direction. There might be several obstacles in the path, but if you enjoy the journey, the road to success can be a pleasurable thing to traverse rather than a donkey's errand.

Single-mindedness

"To succeed in your mission, you must have single-minded devotion to your goal."
– A P J Abdul Kalam

What do we understand by this? Our devotion and single-minded efforts towards our chosen goals can help us reach them and become successful people. Unwavering devotion to the good cause, as inferred by our minds, is a sure-fire way of achieving the goal irrespective of the hurdles in the path, either placed by fate or the pig-headedness of other lesser and envious mortals. Our will and our dedication to triumph can ease our approach towards the goals we have set for ourselves.

Vince Lombardi rightly says: "The difference between a successful person and other is not a lack of strength, not a lack of knowledge, but rather a lack of will."

What do we understand by this? This means that our self-determination is what gives us an upper hand. I might add here that the will has to be free from all inputs because only from absolute freedom, can the choice to be successful be born.

Our self-determination gives us the liberty to choose and command over our decisions. That's why they need free will. We must understand that when our efforts towards our goals are single-minded and full of determination, our inner strength and courage increase manifolds as both are interrelated and directly impact each other. And this leads to strengthening our internal beliefs, which helps us take upon any challenge with confidence and aplomb. An indomitable will is the biggest asset on the high road to success.

Fortitude

> *"Whatever the mind can conceive and believe,*
> *it can achieve."*
> *-Napoleon*

We know that our mind-set sets the initial roadblocks we face while trying to achieve our goals. This mind-set is brought into being by past conditioning. If there isn't much success in the background, there may be a certain tentativeness about prospects, but this can be easily overcome if one is flexible and not rigid in mind. If we lack confidence and self-assurance, things become problematic from the very start of the process. On the other hand, if our reason and vision are apparent and we know exactly what we wish to achieve, our mental blocks automatically dissolve. So, one of the essential ingredients for success is having oodles of self-confidence and grit.

We must remember that if we lack confidence and are not convinced of our capabilities and potential, we will most likely face hurdles that might stop us from dead in our tracks. And thus, procrastination might ensue.

Chapter 4

Mental Health Is the Key

"It's up to you today to start making healthy choices. Not choices that are just healthy for your body, but healthy for your mind."
-Steve Maraboli

A healthy mental state will help you leverage your innate skills and abilities to achieve the success you seek and to live a purposeful life because, ultimately, everything is just a state of mind. A beggar on the streets may be happier within himself than the millionaire riding in his luxurious car past him, weighed down by the innate envy and will to do better than his rivals, plotting and planning how to step on other's shoulders in the quest to be considered successful by the very same people. This is no way to achieve happiness. If success leads to a whole lot of misery due to the methods employed, then such endeavours should be well avoided because they may mess up our minds in inconceivable ways.

We all talk about good physical health and its importance on our path towards success. And it's often remarked that without good health, we can stagnate, and our progress can become stilted; but a sharp, active mind can still be your saving grace in times when your natural vigour runs out. People talk about physical and mental health as if there is a difference between the two. These are just part of one whole entity and very much interrelated. If we are physically fit, then mental health is assured and vice versa unless there are extraneous reasons. If physical fitness is not there, our mental health and capacity might dwindle, and the results can be disastrous.

Without some emotional, analytical, and comprehension abilities, one can have many difficulties, not only in professional but also in personal life. This can lead to the proliferation of complications and uncertainties in life, which our faculties may not be able to survive. So, it's safe to say that physical and mental health also helps us attain and sustain an equilibrium, which in turn supplements our pursuit to achieve what we aspire for in life. Therefore, a balanced approach is imperative wherein we know the importance of physical and mental fitness and the desire to work at their optimum level.

When our mental fitness is at its peak, we can reap its benefits in personal and professional domains. We have more mental strength to face difficult situations, and our minds can cope well. We can face obstacles and ordeals with strength and courage rather than running away from the same. Our mental capabilities are helped immensely by good physical fitness, so the aspiration should be to be physically active to have a good mindset. This will help us sort out our problems and triumph in our battle with anger or sadness.

Nurturing our mental well-being also helps us fight against specific mental health problems that can sometimes lead to chronic conditions. This can be avoided to a large extent by being physically active and partaking in optimum nutrition in a balanced diet. It can also avert the beginning or relapse of a physical or mental illness.

We all know that life can throw many complications and predicaments which can shake our very existence to the core. However, having a good mindset can give us the requisite strength to overcome life's unjust and very idiotic situations. If life throws you a lemon, one should know how to make lemonade; otherwise, life can overwhelm us with its myriad nonsensical rigmarole. To face and tackle such hardships, a healthy and robust mind, along with a healthy body, is a boon. And if we talk about success, it's not a joyride. A lot of intelligence and willpower is needed to attain one's goals.

So, robust mental health is directly proportional to success. If we are not dynamic and ambitious at the same time, we might be inclined to let go of our dreams the moment a failure strikes us, which is a foolish way to be life tries to overwhelm us, but indomitable will can see us through the most testing times and triumph in the end. A determined and healthy mind can help us come out of such feelings of despair and depression that external situations can many times heap upon us. Some measures that can be used to maintain a healthy mind are as follows-

Give voice to your feelings

Good mental health is synonymous with coming out with your feelings and emotions. Sometimes just talking about our troubles can help immensely. When you talk about your perceptions and apprehensions, you find a door opened towards resolutions, provided the other person is supportive and helpful to our cause. Internalizing troubles can have a detrimental effect on mental health; that's why psychiatrists first encourage one to talk about the problem. If you are feeling troubled due to any reason, talking shall help. Keeping emotions locked inside can harm our mental health and may lead to significant problems in the long run.

Many people assume that talking about our feelings is a sign of weakness, but it's quite contrary to this assumption. Coming out with unresolved issues that are bothering us is not wrong. On the contrary, our mental well-being should be of prime importance for us. Talking can open ways to tackle complications and uncertainties, which might be the reason behind our lazy ways, which might affect our output. Being listened to by people we trust, can remove some baggage, and assure us of being supported. And this might help the other person we trusted to open as well.

It's not easy to construe our feelings with ease but trying and sharing our emotions can help us maintain a healthy outlook towards life.

It's not necessary that we can't talk to anyone out of our family circle. Sometimes we are more comfortable talking and sharing our thoughts and feelings with people outside this circle, but who are close and trusted. But one thing is essential: we should never stress ourselves to talk but should let conversations flourish spontaneously and intrinsically. This will ease the awkwardness and help us come out of our shells.

Importance of an active regimen

The streaming demeanour. What do we understand by this phrase?

A river that is flowing continuously has fresh, clean water to begin with. Once it stops flowing, the water turns into its swampy version. The same applies to the human body and mind. When we lead an active life with regular exercise and physical training, our brain releases certain chemicals which make us feel good. Not only this, but regular exercise also keeps our body fit and healthy, which helps in boosting our self-confidence and self-assurance. Our concentration levels rise, and we feel on top of the world with better sleep.

Exercising also keeps our vital organs healthy, leading to a robust body and mind. Walking, cycling, gardening, gym training, running, or playing any sport are all ways of keeping oneself active. That's why in Indian culture, we have Yoga and Pranayama as a daily routine in most people's lives. So, we can opt for the activity we like and make it a part of our daily routine.

Being well-nourished

Having a properly balanced diet that is full of nutrition and is alimentative can be another critical point of discussion. There's an old saying that goes like this," We become what we eat." This doesn't mean that if we eat lettuce and tomatoes, we will become lettuce or tomatoes. It means that if we eat a nutritious diet, it will lead to a healthy body and help maintain great mental strength and vitality.

Our eating habits can have a lasting impact on our inner health, which is directly related to our mental health and makeup. So, for example, if we are highly addicted to sugary foods and snacks or, let's say caffeinated drinks, it can lead to deprivation of specific nutrients for our brain, which is needed to keep it sharp. Sugar can give us an immediate high that's followed by a low, plus it's full of calories and can cause accumulation of fats in the body, so minimal sugar intake is needed to remain healthy. In addition, bad food choices can lead to lethargy and a lack of attentiveness.

Therefore, a balanced diet is compulsory for maintaining good physical health and mental health as well, as both are interrelated. A healthy and balanced diet includes fresh fruits and vegetables, legumes and grains, seeds and nuts, dairy products, etc. We should also include plenty of water in our daily dietary routine as it's imperative to flush out toxins from our bodies. Having at least three full meals every day should become a routine for us and limit high caffeine and sugary food items. Those who drink alcoholic beverages must drink sensibly. We must consult our dietician or doctor to advise us on the specific dietary routine. Every individual is different, and what is needed by one person might not be suitable for the other.

Drink discretely

This is for those who rely on alcoholic drinks to deal with emotional complications and troubles in life. Some drink because of loneliness, and others to forget certain painful happenings. But one thing that we forget is that the effect of alcohol is not permanent, and once the impact of drink wears off, we feel even worse than before, and the withdrawal symptoms lead to a deplorable condition of body and mind. Therefore, if we think that alcohol can help us tackle some issues, we are mistaken. Too much alcohol can not only damage our body organs but can also lead us to self-destruction mode. Therefore, light drinking occasionally is always better than heavy drinking regularly; a couple of drinks per day has been proven to enhance longevity by the beneficial effect on our heart and blood flow in the body. So, it's always better to limit the intake of alcohol.

Apart from this, certain people use other substances when they cannot cope with the mental pressures of life, but again, the effects are short-lived, and the damages are long-term. One should never forget that whether it's alcohol, nicotine, or drugs, they can't solve our problems. Sometimes life promotes such addiction by creating ceaseless troubles; if we always give in to the impulses, then substance addiction follows. This can lead to us being side-tracked from our quest to ultimately triumph over life, irrespective of its various shenanigans. Drugs, alcohol, etc., can only provide us with a temporary relief that comes back to hound once the effects recede. Therefore, substance abuse can sabotage our mental sanity and lead to various physical ailments.

Be in touch with family and friends

Having a supportive family and caring, understanding friends is no less than a boon for anyone. Strong ties with family members help us deal with tensions and strains of life. We can get through any difficulty if we have our loved ones by our side and that can happen only if we are inclusive in our approach. Keeping all our problems to ourselves can sometimes become detrimental to finding solutions. Our family and friends can share their perspectives with us, and this can sometimes help us find resolutions with ease.

Being in touch with people who care for us and sharing our feelings and emotions with them can resolve many problems without much mental stress. Communication is the key. The lines to heartfelt conversations should always remain open. This will help us come out with the issues bothering us and guide us with the respective solutions.

Nothing wrong in seeking help

Life is full of ups and downs and because of tiring life occurrences, feeling overwhelmed or out of place sometimes is no big deal. But the most crucial thing in this scenario is asking for help. If we feel helpless at any point in time and things start getting too much for us to handle, we must seek help, whether it's from a family member, friend, or professional services. There are innumerable counsellors who offer professional help when going through tough times. Such sessions can help us understand the problem better and find solutions.

There is nothing wrong in seeking professional help regarding our mental health. But, of course, we have a particular thought process in our society when seeking help for our mental well-being. Still, just like any other part of the body, our mind also needs help sometimes, and it's always wise to refer to a mental health expert to diagnose and treat the problem.

Taking some "Me Time" off

We are all so engrossed in our daily lives that we forget about ourselves. We need a break now and then to replenish our lost peace of mind, which is essential for maintaining good mental health. Whether it's a small break from our work commitments, a small break from kitchen chores, or a weekend break, getting some 'me-time' can do wonders. It not only de-stresses us but also helps us explore ourselves profoundly and passionately. We can try yoga, meditation, and other relaxation exercises during 'my time', or just not do anything we want.

Our body tends to tell us what it wants, and the only thing needed is to understand its language. Having a good sleep is also very important for sound mental health as the tired and stressed body can be harmful to overall well-being, including mental health.

Indulging in activities we like

Everyone has certain hobbies and interests. We should ask ourselves what we like to do, or better to say what we love to do. Some people like painting, others like gardening and so on. We should try indulging in activities that help in mental relaxation and unwinding. This helps in loosening up and beating stress and boosts our self-esteem and confidence. A distraction can undoubtedly do wonders if we are suffering because of overthinking or feeling stressed due to some inevitable circumstances. What can be a better distraction than indulging in an activity we like!

Accepting ourselves as we are

We are all unique in our way, and no two people are alike. Some are jovial and make people laugh without much effort, some are fabulous cooks, and some are born with problem-solving skills. Some of us are extroverts and like to share our lifestyle and time with people around us, while some of us are introverts who don't feel comfortable in the company of strangers and want to be with people who comprise their inner circle. We are all different in one way or the other. And the most important thing here is acceptance. If we try to ape others to be like them, keeping aside the fact that we all have a different inner makeup, we will suffer.

We have to love ourselves the way we are. This will not only boost our self-confidence but will also help us in having a clearer perspective about ourselves and others. There's nothing wrong with admiring others and wanting to learn new skills and improving knowledge, but not at the cost of changing our core personality. Suppose we still feel that certain aspects of our character should be commutated, contemplating what we need to change about ourselves and whether we intend to bring that change is feasible. In that case, small and gradual steps can be taken to transition. Finally, and most importantly, loving oneself and one's attributes is essential to love others and their qualities.

Living in the moment

Life is an amalgamation of good and bad experiences which leave a deep impression on our inner self. Sometimes we give more importance to what is in the past than in the present. This is because we like to live in what has already passed. But if this becomes a habit, it can ruin our present. If we keep on reliving the moments that might have hurt us or left us with some deep gashes, we will never be able to enjoy our present, and all this will spoil our coming future.

We can take help from a counsellor if needed, or else we can talk it out with people we trust. Living in the moment is the key to a bright future.

Chapter 5

Embracing Your Failures

"If there were no night, we would not appreciate the day, nor could we see the stars and the vastness of the heavens. We must partake of the bitter with the sweet. There is a divine purpose in the adversities we encounter every day. They prepare, they purge, they purify, and thus they bless."
-James E. Faust

Life is seldom a one-tone experience, it keeps surprising us with twists and turns, a suspense thriller with a dash of laughter, love, happiness, and even traumatic situations that leave us distraught and in despair. In the US, the saying goes, life is tough. Indeed, it's forever biting most people springing one nasty surprise after another. From an individual's point of view, it can seem like nothing more than a series of disasters; even when the going seems reasonable, it can spring a nasty surprise out of nowhere for no rhyme or reason. To expect appropriate behavior from life seems like the most outrageous thing. The best anyone can hope to do, is to ride out the stormy interludes of life and pounce on the opportunity that will invariably present itself at some point.

We plan and implement our schemes and ideas with certain expectations, but the injustice of life can send everything haywire. Even when the going is smooth, the nasty surprise is just around the corner. Life is supposed to be bittersweet, but often, the balance is tilted overwhelmingly towards the bitter.

We're constantly in pursuit of our desires with a twinge of passion and enthusiasm. No one likes to fail, but failure seems more guaranteed than success. To be number one is everyone's favourite reward, and it might seem achievable, but it's rarely guaranteed; that's the fickleness of existence. So, failure is much more a possibility than victory.

So how do you deal with it? There are some ways, of course, but the most critical step is to change our perspective of failure from impending doom to a prospect of growth. It's best to consider failure the steppingstone to success, especially if one can pinpoint the exact reason for the failure, then one can learn from past mistakes and hence not repeat them in future endeavors. It's necessary to stop agonizing over failure and look at it as it is – a momentary setback, giving you enough room to restart and bounce back unless a series of disasters overwhelm you then it's best to look incessantly for a reason thereof, or we may be doomed to repeat the same cycle of disasters repeatedly.

Once we know what caused the failure in the first place, it then becomes easier to pre-empt the same things from happening the next time around. When we look at it as the end of the world, we unintentionally dwell upon our fears and tribulations rather than setting up a game plan for future endeavors. We tend to focus on lamenting our plight and, thus, cannot decode our mistakes and follies. But to convert every failure into success, we must inspect and scrutinize ourselves so that we can know where we might've stumbled. Only then, shall we be able to work in the right direction. Some of the reasons to love our failures are as follows:

Failures help us discover who we are

Apart from what we do and what we have accomplished, we get to know ourselves and our capabilities better once we face failure in life. Undoubtedly, success is something we all want and wish for all the time, but it's the failure that carves the perfect foundation on which the mansion of success stands without letting us imbibe any false egos and self-esteem.

Failure is something that keeps us grounded, with our feet firmly on the ground and our eyes towards the sky. Everyone is made for aspiring for the galaxies of success but can do so only with feet firmly on the basis.

Failures help us restore our humbleness and hones our fair-mindedness

Undoubtedly, success is the favourite child amongst the family named life, but failure helps us remain humble and stray away from ego-based practices helping us grow as well-rounded people. Success in professional life is just one aspect of human existence, but real success comprises both professional and humane matters. So, failures can help us carve a better and resolved version of ourselves.

Failures help us in the creation of new ideas and opportunities

When we fail, we know where we went wrong and what not to repeat in the future. We also contemplate the right path to take, whether we wish to carry on with the same thing or take up a new approach. Our horizon increases, so does our vision.

Failures have a subtle effect on us as a person

Failures make us more mature and our resilience to face obstacles and ordeals increases manifolds. As a result, we can digest life with an open mind which helps us in our future endeavors.

Failures lead us to make and change our plans

Once we have faced failures, we can check the moves that lead to the missteps to make new plans or correct them. We can make appropriate rectifications to our ideas and ways of implementation. This helps us stay focused on the target and gives us a fresh perspective and understanding of our approach.

Failures lead to a rendezvous with kindness and generosity

Being kind and compassionate is something we all miss sometimes. We are so engrossed in our liabilities, a professional rat-race, or a financial rut, that we fail to be kind towards others as well as ourselves. Through failures, we have an opportunity to become more considerate and respectful towards everyone around us, including ourselves.

Failures help us understand the value of patience in life

We all know that patience is a virtue, but how often do we practice the same?

Failure often forces us to become more patient and understanding, honing this skill, so that we're able to tackle things in a patient and composed manner, in our future pursuits or life in general.

So, hating our failures is but a futile process that increases agony and does nothing much else. But understanding and learning from our failures is when our life changes. We need to make them the milestone in our journey towards success. If we have this kind of approach, we will never lose heart and dedication towards accomplishing our goals. Let's sum it up with a famous quote by one of the most famous athletes in the world.

> *"I've failed over and over and over again in my life, and that is why I succeed."*
> *-Michael Jordan*

Our wounds can heal and inspire us to achieve what we always wanted to. Our failures can give us the motivation to do better. It all depends on how we perceive our losses, whether we work hard and get rid of all the obstacles and flaws in our approach or give it all up.

Chapter 6

I Will Survive

"Victory is always possible for the person who refuses to stop."
-Napoleon Hill

What signifies a fighting spirit? Well, in layman's language, anyone who doesn't give up, come what may, has a spirit of a warrior.

Our spirit is what defines us and our journey. Throughout our allotted time on this planet, we endure various experiences. Some are delicious, and some quite unsavoury. Good occurrences make us happy, while difficult ones have a different impact on different people. It is often said that anyone can tread the most straightforward course of life, but it's the difficult ones that test one's true mettle.

We come across a lot of advice suggesting that the power of being resilient and maintaining grit and persistence while facing difficulties in life is key to true success. However, we can still find a legitimate answer to the question as to how to maintain that and from where to learn these qualities. We know that we need to shrug off enormous challenges thrown at us by life, keep our persistence intact, and emerge as a winner for success. But the question arises, how? Let's find out our answer through the following insights and some inspirational life journeys.

Observe, Recognise and Consider

When facing trying situations where our endurance is tested, we must keep our guards up. This means that we should learn to observe what is happening around us. Whether our professional or personal situation, it's always better to be prepared for any untoward happening while maintaining a positive demeanour.

Once we are in the right state of mind, where we can perceive and believe that things can go wrong, we can tackle problems better. And of course, the lessons that we acquire along this course become our guide for the future and help us become more resilient. One of the most important things that needs to be tackled is denial.

Yes, it's difficult to accept things that can or are about to go wrong, as this is something we all have encountered at some of the other points in time, but what separates people with an engraved survival instinct from those who give up easily is transitioning from denial to acceptance. This gives them time to perceive situations, come up with solutions, and help their minds move through repudiation, exasperation, and melancholy to acknowledgment quickly.

Living in denial or oblivion can make matters worse. It's not that we have to be paranoid all the time but being prepared for any situation builds a better chance for success and reduces the fear of failure all at the same time. Those who do not give upscale mountain tops, no matter how the journey was.

Foresee Challenges

An eagle can foresee when a storm is approaching long before it breaks?

Instead of hiding, the eagle will fly to some high point and wait for the winds to come. When the storm hits, it sets its wings so that the wind can pick it up and lift it above the storm. So, while the storm rages below, the eagle soars above it.

The eagle does not escape or hide from the storm; instead, it uses the storm to lift it higher. It rises on the stormy winds which others dread.

When the storm of life or challenges hits us, we can rise above them and soar like the eagle that rides the storm's winds. Don't be afraid of the storms or the challenges in your life. Use it to lift you higher in your life.

Slice of Inspiration

Sonam Wangchuk (Engineer, Innovator, Education reformist)

His extraordinary life was the inspiration behind '3 Idiots', a viral Bollywood film.

Wangchuk was considered a stupid child in his early years due to his lack of responsiveness to his teachers and peers. But, later, he completed his education from Delhi and pursued B-Tech from NIT Srinagar. However, he had to finance his education due to the lack of consent of his father over his decision to study. He also completed two years of higher studies in Earthen Architecture from France.

During his graduation, he founded the Students' Educational and Cultural Movement of Ladakh (SECMOL) in 1988 for the 'victims (children)' of an alien education system foisted on Ladakh. He also became the founding director of the revolutionary school, which admitted the kids written off as failures by society. Wangchuk's sole intent was to make learning fun and practical rather than subjecting kids to rote learning. He came into popularity in 2009, when his story inspired Aamir Khan's character Phuntsok Wangdu or Rancho in the Rajkumar Hirani-directed film '3 Idiots'.

Later, his ground-breaking innovations like 'Ice Stupas' and solar heated mud huts put him on the global radar for finding sustainable solutions in challenging terrains.

Manage Your Sentiments and Responses

In his book 'The Survivor Personality', Al Siebert writes that "The best survivors spend almost no time, especially in emergencies, getting upset about what has been lost, or feeling distressed about things going badly.... For this reason, they don't usually take themselves too seriously and are therefore hard to threaten."

We know that it's easier said than done. When facing a problem in life, we feel hysterical and react with our emotions. But sometimes, this can make wrong decisions while handling the issues. Emotions and instincts cannot deal with all troubles.

A study showed that some scuba divers who had oxygen and perfectly functional regulators in their tanks, had shockingly pulled the regulators out of their mouths and thus, drowned. But when we think about this scenario, how is this even possible? Why would someone sabotage themselves in such a gruesome manner? According to researchers, the answer lies in the panic reaction.

When they felt trepidation because certain people can't handle suffocation that well, they acted according to their instinct and emotional response of uncovering their noses and mouths. To think about it, that was probably an understandable reaction for a being that survives on air but in the wrong place of trouble.

When we're suffering from troubled breathing, the most natural, instinctive response would be removing all interferences around the mouth, but it could potentially become troublesome when that response happens subconsciously.

Therefore, keeping our minds calm when facing difficulties is very important, as hasty decisions are never helpful. This goes for everyday life as well. People with resilience and patience acknowledge troubles, keep their minds calm and composed, assess the situation judiciously, plan action, and initiate it.

Slice Of Inspiration

Vijay Vardhan - UPSC Civil Services with 104th Rank

He failed, not once nor twice but 35 times, before cracking UPSC Civil Services exam with 104th Rank.

Vijay's journey started in 2013 when he came to Delhi after completing his engineering in electronics and communication from Hisar, his hometown. He came to Delhi to prepare for the UPSC Civil Services exam. It took him 6 years and numerous failed attempts to ultimately succeed in his chosen field. In these many years, Vijay appeared for more than 35 government exams which he was unable to crack.

This list included UP-PSC, Haryana PCS, Punjab PCS, SSC-CGL, LIC, NABARD, ISRO, Haryana Excise Inspector, RRB-NTPC, RBI Grade B.

In most of these exams he cleared the prelims but was unable to crack the main exam or interview. At times he failed at the final stage in the medical exam or in the document verification process. But he did not lose his courage and kept going. This not only led to the achievement of his ultimate goal but also become an inspiration to many others.

Leave When the Need Arises

Many of the readers might be feeling a little perplexed. How can quit be a mantra to success? Well, maybe not quitting something entirely but at least taking a break from it, one that might help you readjust your approach and tackle it more effectively.

The assessment of our capabilities and mental strength can play a significant role in building the blocks of our road to success and realizing whether we're up to the challenge or not, is also essential for getting the desired results.

It's always better to take a vacation from something that might destroy us mentally or psychologically (- a terrible defeat, for instance), and come back to it once we've primed up our minds for the potential loss as well. We can equip ourselves with what it takes to win over the situation once we look outside. That's why assessing our abilities and skills, from time to time, is imperative.

Secondly, suppose we feel that some goals that we thought of achieving might be unattainable for various reasons. In that case, rather than running after them headfirst, it's better to quit them and go for what is attainable and adds value to our existence.

According to Dr. Carsten Wrosch, people who leave their unobtainable ambitions show certain physical and psychological benefits. He says," They have, for example, more minor depressive symptoms, less adverse effects over time, they also have lower cortisol levels, and they have lower levels of systemic inflammation, which is a marker of immune functioning. And they develop fewer physical health problems over time."

So, it's safe to say that although going after what we want is essential to winning, sometimes taking stock and critical thinking is also necessary to help us decide what we should be going after and what we should leave, which might help us win even more effectively.

Slice of Inspiration

Allyson Felix, American Track and Field Athlete, an entrepreneur with her shoe brand, in her initial professional years, Felix specialized in the 200 meters sprint and gradually shifted to the 400 meters sprint. Her racing repertoire spans the 100 meters, 4 x 100 meters relay, and 4 x 400 meters relay.

But it was not a smooth sport for her, and she faced various ligament injuries during her training and complications during her pregnancy. When Allyson Felix got pregnant, Nike offered her 70% less on her contract and told her, "Know your place and just run."

She quit working with Nike and started her running shoes called 'Saysh' with the slogan "I Know My Place." Allyson won 11 medals in the Tokyo Olympics (2020) and emerged as the most sought-after woman sprinter.

Felix currently holds the title of the most decorated athlete, male or female, in the World Athletics Championship history with 18 career medals, seven from individual events, and 11 from team relays. In addition, she was included in Time magazine's 100 Most Influential People 2020 and 2021.

Preparations

It's often said that we should live in the moment, which is essential for a better life experience. Living in the past doesn't serve any purpose, and the future is so far away that it becomes the present by the time you experience follows.

But preparing for the future always helps us when the moment arises. Of course, we can't know precisely what might transpire, but being prepared for the contingencies will never hurt. For example, suppose we work in the corporate. In that case, we can keep preparing for our future life as an entrepreneur or an artist or whatever piques our interest by honing our skills on the fly so that when we're finally ready to leave our present employment or, in a worst-case scenario, we are laid off; we are prepared to take up another one with a better skill set.

The future is a mist as we can never really predict what the next moment might bring us, but good productive habits and a little preparation will help us be more resilient. So, we should always keep expecting the best from our lives, but we must also be prepared for the worst. We ought to be proactive, and rather than waiting for good things to happen, we must create the path that will lead to good things.

Some of the inspiring people who have created a niche for themselves as well as carved a path for others to follow are as follows:

Slice of Inspiration

Milton Hers Comp (An American Chocolatier, Businessman, And Philanthropist.) Founder of the "The Hershey Company"

Milton Hershey was expected to help at their family farm, and he learned the value of hard work and perseverance from a very young age. Henry Hershey, his father, rarely stayed anywhere very long and was prone to leaving his wife and child for long periods. Because of this, Milton had a minimal education with no schooling beyond the 4th grade.

He worked as an apprentice with a printer the was fired due to some mistake. Then he worked as an apprentice in the confectionery shop. Finally, he learned the art of making caramel candies and started three separate candy-related ventures. But to his fate, all of them failed.

Hershey founded the Lancaster Caramel Company in the last-ditch attempt and started seeing tremendous results. After that, he became interested in chocolates and created "The Hershey Company," or simply, Hershey's.

He then formed the "Hershey Industrial School" with a deed of trust and a charitable foundation that provides cultural and educational opportunities to Hershey residents.

There's nothing wrong in asking for help

We all want to evade situations wherein we're forced to ask for help. No one likes to be put into such a predicament. We feel embarrassed or ashamed to ask for assistance as our pride comes in the way.

But we must understand that there's nothing wrong in expecting help from those there for us. We know that we too shall always be there for them and the gesture, often, goes both ways. So, getting help and giving service is a way to bring our society closer. And perhaps it's an act of God himself when those who are going through the most challenging phases of life are willing to step up and help others.

That is because by becoming someone who cares and helps, seeing others struggling, lends a new meaning to our shallow lives, and the feeling of self-worth also increases.

You must've heard about **Leon Weliczker**, a holocaust survivor.

His strength was his dedication to his brother and safety. Leon might not have survived alone. Still, when his fifteen years old brother Aaron came into the picture, Leon felt a surge of love and an undying sense of responsibility. Suddenly emerging from the identity of being a victim, he had adopted the role of the rescuer. When he decided to help his brother, his own belief in surviving became prominent. It helped him rise above his fears.

Similarly, when we feel responsible for others and go out of our way to help them, we ensure our survival. We become more focused and feel a lot more energetic to persevere. This is because we think that we are not doing it only for ourselves, but other souls depend on us. And if life reverses the roles, and we become the ones who need others' help, we can ask the people we are close to us for help. There is nothing wrong with that. And once the dust of trying situations settles, life becomes more apparent. We also understand the difference between real and fake people.

Slice of Inspiration

Rajat Sharma Host of the show "Aap Ki Adalat"

(A 2015 Padma Bhushan winner for his contributions in the field of Journalism.)

Rajat came from a family with humble beginnings. His father could not afford expensive education for his children, so Rajat went to a community school. The family struggled to make ends meet. Rajat Sharma used to go to his neighbours' house to watch TV. Because they did not own a television set.

He studied hard and got into Shri Ram College of Commerce. His college senior, Shri Arun Jaitley, became an inspiration for his life and even helped him with the fees.

In 1992, he bumped into Zee TV's Subhash Chandra during a flight, and it was amid a casual conversation that the concept of Aap Ki Adalat took shape. By that time, Rajat Sharma had successfully established himself as an editor and had shifted to Bombay.

In 2004, he started his news channel, India TV, which drained his investments for the first two years. He had to sell off his properties to pay the salaries. However, he did not give up and changed his strategies; accordingly, today, it is one of the most-watched news channels.

Work Hard

When the going gets tough, the best way to survive is to give it all. This helps us sail through rough waters and keeps our emotions in check, which might just be in chaos during trying times. If we talk about how people feel when going through challenging phases, the emotions can get quelled by sadness, distraction, panic, etc. This can lead to getting more and more drenched in an emotional mess. This can only be overcome if we try to keep ourselves distracted by keeping busy. This will help us stay calm during such times and help us keep marching towards our way out of the chaos. So, we must keep working hard rather than sitting idle and thinking about the how, the why, and the why me.

Slice of Inspiration

Kalpana Saroj: Indian Entrepreneur, TEDx Speaker, Chairperson, Kamani Tubes Company.

Her extraordinary life has inspired the makers of the Oscar Award-winning Slumdog Millionaire.

The poster child of going from rags to riches through the display of sheer will, grit, and determination, Kalpana Saroj is a true inspiration to youngsters around the world. Born in the Roperkheda Village in Maharashtra, she was married off by her parents at 22 years. She faced physical abuse during her first marriage at the hands of her husband and his parents. She even tried to commit suicide.

Saroj is a Buddhist who was inspired by and followed the teachings of Dr. Ambedkar. She started helping the scheduled caste communities by taking loans from the government and then gradually started her own tailoring business and then a furniture business. Soon she bought the assets of Kamani Tubes Company and turned the loss-making company into a highly lucrative business.

She then built up a successful real estate business and became known for her contacts and entrepreneurial skills. Kalpana Saroj was also awarded the Padma Shri for Trade and Industry in 2013. In addition, she was appointed as one of the Board of Directors of Bhartiya Mahila Bank, a bank primarily for women, by the Government of India. She also serves on the Board of Governors of IIMB.

Now we know that we can come out of the most challenging situations with sustained and consistent efforts. All we need to do is to gather ourselves and work towards triumph by never losing hope and moving forward in life.

Chapter 7

Surrender (To) Your Dreams

"Never give up on a dream just because of the time it will take to accomplish it. The time will pass anyway."
-Earl Nightingale

We all have dreams. Sometimes these dreams get accomplished efficiently, and sometimes they seem hard to realize. When we cannot get what we aspire for, we either blame our luck or pin it on destiny. Sometimes we abuse the Almighty, too, putting the onus on him. But aren't those who show courage and resilience during distressing times the ones who manage to uphaul the sails of their lives?

So many people have stood firm in the face of adversities have created history. And there are millions more, who are silently and consistently fighting the good fight, trying to better themselves to reach the shore of success.

So, what demarcates those that achieve their dreams and those that don't?

Maybe it's their "Never Say Never" attitude, their persistence, their determination, or perhaps it's the sheer grit that never lets them sleep in the pursuit of their passion. Such people realize their dreams with aplomb and become an inspiration for many others who are going through rough terrain.

What about luck? Sure, to some extent, of course. But then, even if a chance is on our side, and we relax and doze off, forgetting to put in the necessary efforts, success shall remain a dream only. Difficulties can indeed bring untoward stress in life, but sometimes the only way to come out of the rut is to continue striding through it. Struggles can either be *The End* or a life lesson, the choice is ours. But there is no need to fret or go into a shell and suffer. Instead, make your move, learn your lesson, and March ahead.

Our brains are wired to keep us protected, and this is simply how we've always been. So, survival will always be the most imperative goal for our monkey brain.

Sometimes this leads to our consciousness deliberately sabotaging our dreams, as our minds might calculate the risk to be too big or too daunting, and it's better to stay snuggled within our comfort zone anyway. This happens when we imagine our dreams to be an impossible feat. However, we also know that great things call for outstanding efforts. Averageness might bring you average results, but one needs to ignite a great fire to surmount an extraordinary mountain.

The first step is to tighten up your seatbelt and enjoy the roller coaster ride. We might face obstacles and ordeals, which might break our spirit, making us apprehensive about our strengths and attributes, but we must remember that one failure cannot decide the course of our life. It's there to teach us something precious—a lesson for life which might change us in the most delicious way possible.

Give Yourself - 'Some Time'

It's not right to pressurize oneself while striving to achieve the goal one is aspiring for. Always remember, the great wall of

China wasn't made in a single day and the Eiffel tower was made in 2 years 2 months and 5 days. What do you think would've happened, if the ones constructing these beautiful wonders were pressurized to finish fast? It would've resulted in failure. In the same way, it takes time to comprehend things so that the right action is taken. Even if it takes a bit longer to fulfil your dreams, don't give up. Give yourself some time and consideration. It will surely work out.

Create a Blueprint

Everything that is planned perfectly goes smoothly. We should never go out with half-baked ideas that can ruin the opportunities for growth and success. Being proactive always helps. This not only prepares us well before the actual challenge appears, but also gives us time to explore other options to reach our goal as well.

Not Getting Perturbed Because Of Failure

Ups and downs make life, and positivity helps slide through complicated messy situations without harming the sanctity of our existence. Keeping one's mental and emotional intelligence intact, even during tough times, can be advantageous in the long run. Analyse, think, and act.

Chapter 8

Some Success Habits

"We are what we repeatedly do. Success is not an act but a habit."
-Aristotle

Are there any habits that can help us achieve what we wish? Yes, why not? If we bring specific needed changes in our ways of dealing with life and its happenings, things might change. Let us have a look at some of the practices that can be adapted.

The Very Best for The Very Best

If we want the best in life, we must give it our best. Efforts go a long way, and most give off positive results. But, if we keep making meek efforts, without much enthusiasm, we will get results that are less than what we want.

Finding The Finest Way Possible

When we feel hungry, do we wait for food to automatically appear to satisfy our hunger? No, we try. We find food, cook it if needed and eat it. Then why do we wait around for the best way possible to reach our goals? We should expand the horizons of our dedication to diligently create our future instead of waiting for good things to happen automatically in life. Instead of putting all our energies into grappling with setbacks and waiting for better opportunities, we should shift some points into creating a better reality.

Everything Needs Revamping at Some Point of Time

This applies to our personal development as well. Like we prioritize saving for the future as our long-term financial goal, we need to prioritize self-guided improvements that can help us evolve into a better version of ourselves, who can face all challenges easily.

Self-Care Is Important

The only person we care for the least is ourselves. We must remember that we are responsible for this body and mind and taking care of its health and wellness should be on top of our to-do list. Regular exercise and a healthy regime can be very beneficial in the long run. A healthy mind and a healthy body are all that we need to overcome the hurdles and roadblocks to reach our destination.

Time: The Most Precious Asset

We all know that time, once wasted, never comes back. Time is money. We can earn money again, but if time is not properly utilized, is gone forever. So, we should make sure that we make good use of it by spending it on things that will help us in our personal life and professional growth.

When Actions Align with Words, Trust Flourishes

Trust is earned through actions. We all know how fragile trust is. It takes minutes to break and years to mend again. And even fixed, the same is akin to a crumpled piece of paper. So, we should always take care of the trust others show in us and invest our trust only in people we think shall be able to guard it well.

Keep Updating Knowledge

Knowledge always pays. For that, it's good to be an avid reader. Whenever we read, we absorb pearls of wisdom that might be useful at some point of time in life.

Every Action Has Consequences

We all know that our actions have repercussions. Going haywire with unplanned activities can jeopardize our journey towards our goals. It's always best to decide what we want to do and then work out an action plan. That way, we can avert some clumsy unplanned moves and unwanted results.

Learning is A Lifelong Undertaking

Life is a stringent teacher who teaches till our last breath. We should always refrain from thinking that we know everything. This stifles our prospects of growing and makes our knowledge stale and mushy like stagnant water. We can attain knowledge through various means, like reading, being attentive towards the happenings around us, sustained efforts to keep ourselves updated with the current scenario and developments in our field and socio-political issues, not only in our own country but throughout the world. We should keep learning as life never fails to teach.

Maintain A Balance

Life is all about maintaining a balance. And it's not something we inherit, but it's something we create. Therefore, it's always best to prioritize things. This helps you find a well-designed way to distribute your time and efforts and enables you to get through life smoothly.

Humility Pays

It's always good to stay humble, even if we have accomplished a lot in life. Even when they have everything, a humble person is successful in the true sense. Humility is the foundation on which all other virtues stand firm.

Think Positive, Be Positive

Positivity flows inside people who have a cheerful demeanour. So, it's better to stay away from negative people, as their toxicity can influence our minds in the wrong manner. With a spirit to create a beautiful future and live a fantastic present, we must try to remain positive, even when things are difficult. This will help us with a foothold to come out of any situation. So be positive through good and bad times.

Tough Times Don't Last, But Tough People Do

We must not lose hope and should not let our efforts diminish, even when facing tough times. It's our patience and resilience that pull us out through such trying times. We must learn the art of accepting a difficulty, understanding it well, and then plan for a solution.

Remove The Need for External Validation

"So long as you are still worried about what others think of you, you are owned by them. Only when you require no approval from outside yourself can you own yourself."
-Oprah Winfrey

Confidence is an asset. If we are not confident of our abilities and skills, no one will be. Therefore, we need to march confidently in the direction of our dreams. The tendency of people-pleasing and looking at them for approval never helps. We must replace these habits by believing in ourselves.

Gratitude Is Directly Proportional to Happiness

"We learned about gratitude and humility – that so many people had a hand in our success."
-Michelle Obama

It's perfectly alright to dream big and have high aspirations. But these shouldn't be at the cost of a lack of peace of mind. And peace comes with Gratefulness. So, when we feel grateful for what we already have, we carry on with our journey towards our ambitions and goals with a sense of contentment and pleasure. It also gives us a feeling of tranquillity and mental calmness.

Change, If Need Arises

"Those who cannot change their minds cannot change anything."
-George Bernard Shaw

There is a saying that the trees do not show flexibility during the storm break, break. So, flexibility is an asset that we should all celebrate. Change is the only constant. What is feasible today might become obsolete tomorrow. So, adapting to the present scenario and developments is the key to growth and success.

Ask Away

"Don't be afraid to ask questions. Don't be afraid to ask for help when you need it. I do that every day. Asking for help isn't a sign of weakness. On the contrary, it's a sign of strength. It shows you dare to admit when you don't know

something and learn something new"
-Barack Obama

If learning constantly is imperative to growth, there's nothing wrong with settling our doubts if there's something difficult to understand. But rather than keeping it all piled up inside, it's better to come out with our issues.

Learn from Past Mistakes

"If you live long enough, you'll make mistakes. But if you learn from them, you'll be a better person. It's how you handle adversity, not how it affects you. The main thing is never quit, never quit, never quit."
-Bill Clinton

As discussed in an earlier chapter, we should not be ashamed of failures and never regret the wrongs. Instead, mistakes should be taken as a learning experience so that what we learn from them is never repeated in the future.

Make Success a Passion, Not an Obsession

"Passion is a positive obsession. Obsession is a negative passion".
-Paul Carvel

We must be passionate about their dreams and goals, and success should be something that inspires us, but we should never make success our obsession. There's a fine line between being consumed by our passions and obsessed with them. Most of us are unable to distinguish between the two. The idea is to ensure we have a supportive railing that safeguards us from being plagued by a desire for success, leading to self-destruction. No doubt, obsession might make one successful in worldly measures. Still, it can also hinder and destroy growth velocity, leading to inaccurate decision-making and illogical reasoning in the long run. We should be passionate about success as this will motivate us to become successful and help us remain sound and grounded.

Don't Let Success Play a Different Ball Game in Your Mind

"Don't let success go to your head and failure to your heart."

-Will Smith

Who doesn't like success? Everyone does. But we should make sure not to let success drive us crazy. Accepting failures with faith and success with humility should be our motto. This will never let our feet move off the ground while aspiring for the stars. A person who gets swayed when success knocks at the door and becomes arrogant and disdainful of others can never understand the true meaning of success. Only a balanced person knows how to remain the same when being showered by the rains of prosperity during good times and facing failures during adverse times.

Chapter 9

Keep Away from Negatives in Life

"We can complain because rose bushes have thorns or rejoice because thorn bushes have roses."
-Abraham Lincoln

When it comes to Covid-19, a negative result might be positive to hear. But in life, negativities can wreak havoc. Can you imagine a worse situation than being surrounded by negative people, drowning in adverse conditions, or, to top it all off, being engrossed in negative thoughts and feelings? There is no doubt that we do have the capacity to manage our emotions and control our moods to a certain extent. However, our responses to external factors can still be altered to a great degree by these extrinsic elements.

These factors can be harmful as well as positive. While the positives can garner positive reactions and results, the negativities can create a hostile environment that can affect our state of mind and our emotional quotient. Therefore, it's imperative to avoid such triggers that can generate a vehemence to pull us down in the dumps. Keeping oneself away from all such toxic elements that can vandalize our mental and physical well-being is not an easy task. Such toxicity can appear in any form, shape, and size. Whether in our personal or professional lives, we can face negative people and situations. And rather than losing our composure and positive outlook, we should try to remain calm and get through the negativities without getting off our trajectory.

However, unexpected situations can pop up where harmful elements surround us, and we must retain our composure and positive outlook to get through them unaffected. Of course, we all know that it's easier said than done, but we can adopt specific ways to keep away from them and work towards positives in life. This way, we can be a happier and healthier version of ourselves.

Feeling Grateful

"Reflect upon your present blessings—of which every man has many—not on your past misfortunes, of which all men have some."
-Charles Dickens

Gratitude is something that can fortify our emotional well-being in every possible way. When we shift our thoughts and point of convergence from what we don't have, to what we've been blessed with, there's a surge in positive energy. Our brain starts noticing the abundance in our lives, making us feel happy and content. This doesn't mean that we must stop dreaming of other goals that we wish to accomplish, but by imbibing gratitude in our lives, we will start valuing what we already have, and this will instil emotional and mental strength, which will, in turn, inspire us even more. So, whenever we're feeling low, we must think of something that we are grateful for. This will keep negative thoughts away and give way to positive notions and beliefs.

Practicing Condonation

"Anger begets more anger, and forgiveness and love lead to more forgiveness and love."
-Lord Mahaveer

Holding grudges can be detrimental to one's peace of mind. It's like carrying a sack full of pains and agonies. The best way to avoid negativity is to let go. By forgiving others and ourselves, we get rid of old resentments and grievances and get a clean slate to start over again. This gives us a chance to truly love ourselves and others without any prior baggage.

Living In the Present

"The past is history. The future is a mystery. This moment is a gift; this moment is called the present. Enjoy it"
-Alan Johnson

Life is an amalgamation of all kinds of memories and dreams. Some memories bring happiness, and some remind us of the pains we endured. One of the most pertinent reasons for negativity to arise is, dwelling through the memories reminding of the past happenings, especially the hurtful ones. When we meditate about such painful moments, we relive them to some extent. And when it comes to the future, that is indeed a mystery that no one knows. So rather than living in the past or guessing about the end, it's better to live in the present. We should look around and enjoy what we have today rather than sulking about past events. This will give us immense peace of mind and help us create a foundation for a better future.

Give Yourself Some Well-Deserved Breaks

"Do something nice for yourself today. Find some quiet, sit in stillness, breathe. Put your problems on pause. You deserve a break".
-Akiroq Brost

Aspiring for big things in life is not wrong. Everyone has dreams, and one has to make an effort to realize these dreams. But one should never forget to be thoughtful towards one's own mental and emotional well-being. Taking small "exuberance breaks" can help us rejuvenate, which in turn can brings positivity and a renewed spark of energy to our lives. Taking good care of ourselves by imbibing specific positive patterns and practices in our daily routine shall keep negative thoughts at bay and generate positive energy to pursue our life goals with happiness.

Penning Down Goals, We Wish to Achieve

"If we have a goal and a plan and are willing to take risks and make mistakes and work as a team, we can choose to do the hard thing."
-Scott Kelly

Our brains functions in a certain way, in which it adapts to the intentions we set for ourselves. So, writing down what we wish to achieve in life increases our chances of achieving them. As a result, our mind gets a lot more motivated and enthusiastic towards the goals, their accomplishment, and the subsequent happiness that comes from the same, and the most exciting part is that the journey becomes enjoyable and memorable.

Never Indulge in Negative Self Talk

"Turn down the volume of your negative inner voice and create a nurturing inner voice to take its place. Forgive yourself, learn from it, and move on instead of obsessing about it when you make a mistake. But, equally important, don't allow anyone else to dwell on your mistakes or shortcomings or to expect perfection from you."
-Beverly Engel

No matter who we are and whose company we get to enjoy, most of our lives are spent on our own, so talking to your lifelong best friend is only natural. Alone or surrounded, in a happy mood, or engulfed in sadness, we're consistently conversing with ourselves in an easy or a catch-22 situation. And there's something therapeutic about it because the way we know ourselves, no one else in the world does But the problem arises when the negative voice takes over and starts sabotaging our plans. So, this is its way to safeguard us from getting hurt or failing.

It happens only when we don't believe in ourselves or feel scared to move ahead. Whenever the negative voice tries to influence our minds, it's imperative to reassure ourselves that we are capable enough to get ahead in life. The day we start acknowledging our strength and conditioning, we will stop indulging in self-doubt. Life is an amalgamation of success and failure, and a handful of losses cannot become our introduction card. So, we need to believe in ourselves and learn to nip negative self-talk on its bud.

Avoid the Company of Negative People

Negative people will sometimes:

*Demean Your Value.

*Destroy your Image

*Drive you crazy!

*Disregard your Dreams

*Discredit your Imagination!

*Defame your Abilities, and

*Disbelieve your Opinions!

Stay away from negative people!

Whether in our professional life or personal, it's good to stay away from negative people. Of course, it's not easy to get rid of them, but the least we can do is try. Studies show that individuals trapped in the company of people who showcase negative attributes cannot shine according to their competence. This is because of the innate impact the negative people.

So, keeping a healthy distance is imperative if we can't be away from it. We sometimes notice that there are people with whom we don't feel energetic and enthusiastic. Instead, we feel drained and rinsed. Even when they haven't done anything remotely annoying, this might be because of their underlying negative vibes. So, keeping a distance from such energy vampires and toxic people who spread negativity all around, would only pay off in the long run.

Do What Makes You Happy

"Nothing in life is to be feared, and it is only to be understood. Now is the time to understand more so that we may fear less."
-Marie Curie

When we do something that doesn't seem to work, but is our passion, we don't feel burnt out even for a single day. So, choose what you do in life according to what you want to do. And even if we can't make our passion our profession, we should take time to indulge in it. It will not only give us immense pleasure but will also work as a therapeutic activity. So, leave everything aside whenever you feel bogged down by life, and relish the exercises that strengthen your spirit.

Step Out for Fresh Air

"By all means, never fail to get all the sunshine and fresh air you can."
-Joseph Pilates

Sometimes, fresh air can stimulate better oxygen circulation in our blood, resulting in a surge in positive energy inside our beings. It can also clear our minds of negativity. When we connect with Nature, we automatically feel positive and productive.

Exercise And Yoga

Move your joints every day. First, you must find your tricks. Then, bury your mind deep in your heart, and watch the body move by itself.

We all know that regular exercising sessions are good for our physical health, but these physical activities can take care of our mental and emotional well-being as well. Research shows that people who exercise regularly exhibit low rates of mental illness. Regular exercise helps us sleep better, and a well-rested mind and body are imperative for a positive life experience in general. Exercise can elevate our coping ability and enhance our self-esteem. It distracts our minds from all sorts of negative thoughts and feelings. Training can improve our energy levels as well. We feel more connected to our inner self, which helps us strengthen our elemental composition.

Chapter 10

Self-Expectancy

*"In order to succeed, people need a sense of
Self-efficacy, struggle together with resilience
To meet the inevitable obstacles and
Inequalities of life"*
-Albert Bandura

Whether we realize it or not, all of us have a set of expectations and dreams, either from life, others, or ourselves. These expectations undergo many enhancements and changes throughout our lives, but some of us cannot gather awareness towards what we wish to do or what we want from our experience. This is because the thread of our core belief system lies in our subconscious mind rather than the conscious self. Therefore, our thoughts wander here and there without much attentiveness, due to which we are not able to decide what exactly we want from ourselves.

So, the first step towards realizing what we expect from ourselves, and our lives is the adoption of alertness. Being more alert towards our day-to-day thoughts and feelings shall give us a blueprint of our core beliefs. These underlying beliefs can help us evaluate our concealed expectations, which might be a little blurry. The awareness of thoughts and ideas is essential to understand the core beliefs and simultaneously fulfil what we want.

Sometimes our hidden expectations can be more harmful than good; many of us unknowingly expect life to be difficult and unfair and uninspiring and a struggle. This can result in our unconscious mind attracting things that actualize these expectations in our lives. And we're then left blaming God or the stars and destiny for our misfortunes when our own beliefs are put on display as a clear mirror to our inner world. The only way to change our life is to adjust our expectations consistently, habitually from the world and everything in it.

How can we realize something when that very something is not clear?

We need to prioritize our thoughts and views and the recurring patterns in our lives. Do we understand ourselves and our lives accurately? I'm sure many people will have an affirmative response to this question. But many of us don't.

We keep on moving through our life without knowing what exactly we want from it. Not what our parents want, not what society wants, not what the circumstances we were born and raised in have made us accustomed to enjoying. Our desires, our spirit's true visceral calling. Most of us aren't even aware that what we want has nothing to do with our likes and dislikes but the likes and dislikes we picked up along this journey called life. Hence, like a sheep in a herd, we begin walking towards a dream we were meant to fail in.

Mechanical as it might sound, we keep on moving ahead, not knowing what expectations we have from ourselves and our lives. Caught in the web of pressures forced upon us by societal norms and values, we forget to understand what we want. Rather than working on expectations that we set for ourselves, we start working towards fulfilling expectations set by others to get a specific validation. And this is not only about professional life. Why are we constantly seeking external validation when it comes to personal life? Of course, we have certain people who wish the best for us and always recommend the right things to be done, but that doesn't mean that we should stop putting our minds and hearts to use. There's nothing wrong with listening to our well-wishers, but whatever comes our way should always be contemplated by our thoughts and ideas as well. We should use others' suggestions as an added guideline but keep our cogitations as the benchmark.

Not Putting Ourselves Down

Am I good enough? Will I be able to do this?

Ever had such thoughts? I'm sure, yes. How can we judge ourselves even before we've done something? So many times, we come across such situations where we know what we must do, but we're unable to take the first step because of self-doubt. We doubt ourselves. And this uncertainty crawls in, especially when we have high expectations for ourselves. Due to this, even without trying, we give up. But the question is, why? And why not try before passing such contemplations? We don't only judge others; we believe ourselves as well, and that too before trying. We should adopt a non-judgemental approach while thinking about our capabilities and limitations.

Expectations From Others and Ourselves

Sometimes things are not clear because of the vagueness of our thoughts, this leads to difficulty in decision making. What do we expect from ourselves and others as well? This is the most important and revealing question that we need to ask ourselves. It will not only clear our minds of all the confusions and perplexities but will also aid our minds in taking the right path towards the goal we've set for ourselves. Most of the time, we set very high expectations for ourselves and others, and when the bar is set very high, there are more chances of failing in our own eyes. This doesn't mean that we shouldn't think or aspire for higher goals in life, but one step taken at a time can be more helpful in the long run as we gain experience along the way. Human psychology is not very simple. It's an amalgamation of complexities that can entangle anyone. That is why we must be aware of our thoughts, motivations, and beliefs so as not to feel intertwined. Ask yourself what you wish to accomplish and whether it's reasonable or not. This will help determine the actual benchmark and give a reality check from time to time.

When Passion Becomes Profession

There are so many people around who, despite having accomplished high goals and objectives, are not happy in the true sense. Why is it so? Are they unsatisfied with their respective work or aspiring for something higher? It can be both. But if we are not enjoying what we are doing right now, no matter how many achievements are accomplished, we will not be able to gain real happiness. That is why we see people who are in pursuance of their dreams which complement their passions and choices, as the happiest in comparison to those who are doing something just for the sake of doing.

To sum up, we can try and create a bond with our inner self so that we are able to connect completely with our feelings and thoughts without any foggy or hazy weather. We feel lost only when the path towards our destination is murky, and that is what we mu mantras that we can recit

Chapter 11

The personal success mantras to imbibe

"Believe in yourself. You are beaver than you think, more talented than you know, and capable of more than you imagine."
-Roy T. Bennett

"Believe in yourself. You are braver than you think, more talented than you know, and capable of more than you imagine." — Roy T. Bennett.

Whilst talking about mantras, a holy hymn or a sacred utterance comes to our mind. And somewhere our soul feels connected to this word itself. So are there any mantras for success as well? Perhaps!

The only thing needed here is a dedicated and committed approach. Success is no walk in the park, true, but with sheer will and persistence, even the highest mountains can be scaled. One just needs to continue to follow their plan and things tend to work out. This leads to a happier and inspired self and the feeling escalates our journey further. We become positive and self-motivated with every successful step towards success.

The biggest challenge that a person faces is when things start to go awry. When our plans flounder leading to the bitter taste of failure, it can have devastating effects on our self-confidence and self-esteem. Motivation goes out the window and with each passing day, we feel even more forlorn and dejected. Whilst confronted with such situations, one needs to create his own success mantra and chant it religiously. Not in the way one would chant a religious mantra though, the trick is to really feel into that which you're claiming yourself to be and to embody it till it becomes second nature and success comes knocking on your door, or at least, the willpower and confidence required for success does.

What is the concept of having a personal success mantra?

It isn't rocket science, understood by an elite few. It's a simple equation. An equation between your aspirations, thoughts, and feelings.

Whenever facing hardships, chanting these success mantras can help you come out of the self-loathing zone.

Whenever facing some insurmountable summons to withstand chaos, these mantras can become your aid.

These are good old words weaved together to create a powerful course of action for yourself.

Our thoughts and the thought processes behind them have a lot of power. We become what we think, and these positive affirmations can help one stay positive, even in the midst of the ultimate distress.

Ups and downs maketh life, and positivity helps slide through these complicated, messy situations without harming the sanctity of our existence. A simple mantra" I can do this" might seem unimpressive and rather defenceless against the roller coaster ride of life, but to truly feel into its innate and massive power, it can act like a motivational tool to help us rediscover our confidence and courage. In the same way, a few personal success mantras can help is rediscover our capabilities and potential.

Does having a success mantra work in actuality?

I know everyone would like to ask, do these mantras or affirmations work? Yes and No. Yes, if you believe in them and your worthiness. No, if you don't have faith in it and your capabilities.

If you try it for the sake of trying it whilst debating with yourself if it'll work or not, then it probably won't. A strong belief system is very important. Our subconscious self has a lot of potential. It can make or break situations without any prior notice. Humans are still trying to decode the potentiality of the same. But one thing is for sure, drastic positive shifts can happen by keeping a positive demeanour.

Through these success mantras, we're feeding you subconscious mind all the goodness of positivity and motivation. It is a simple phenomenon, where your thoughts are your guide and it's always good to keep your guide constructive and buoyant. A right frame of mind consisting of balanced amount of essential positivity as well as a zeal to succeed will always help.

Some success mantras that can be adopted today

In one of his interviews, actor Shahrukh Khan, who's one of the most influential and successful actors of all times, told the interviewer that no matter how many struggles he endured or how much of negativity he faced throughout his journey in the filmdom, he continues to remind himself, "I am the best," the first thing in the morning. Isn't it a great mantra to boost one's own self confidence and self-esteem? No amount of criticism or trolling has ever affected him negatively. It's not that he mustn't have faced any problems in life, but his belief in himself helps him tackle difficult situations with ease. Similarly, here are some mantras that can help us:

I am the creator of my life

You need to tell yourself what you want in life. You need to build a strong foundation for a successful life and that is something only you ought to do. Your self-belief shall escalate you towards our goals.

My energy and enthusiasm is always overflowing

Whenever you're feeling low, the feeling tires you mentally and psychologically, even if you're feeling fine physically. This affects your ability to work and resultantly affects the outcome. You should always tell yourself that you are brimming with positive energy and joy in every scene and scenario.

I am bound to make it big in life

The definition of success is different for each one of us. For some it's subjective, and objective for others. Whatever your definition may be, you have to keep that as your goal and tell yourself constantly, that you're made to succeed and make it big in life.

My potential is limitless and my ability to conquer my challenges is boundless

Never underestimate yourself and your potential. The moment you think that you can't do something, you tend to become an obstacle towards your goal by yourself. You have to keep motivating yourself so that there's nothing in the world, that seems unapproachable and difficult to achieve.

My mind is full of positive thoughts and my life is prosperous

It's understandable to not feel positive when things are going south. All sorts of negative thoughts start piling up, making your mind their abode. But these are moments to rise to the occasion, and to tell remind yourself that negativity is a choice and so is trusting in yourself and your calibre.

Remember… "Positive thoughts and emotions shall attract positive results," with constant and consistent efforts!

What I envision, one day my life shall be

We have always been told by our elders that success can't be achieved based on dreams. But without these dreams, how does one know what to achieve? So, you have to create a vision in your mind, and feel into the truth that one day it shall become a reality.

The obstacles in my path are all temporary

One thing that you have to remember is nothing lasts forever. Even obstacles and difficulties are temporary. You have to keep telling yourself that your hard work and dedication shall remove the obstacles, clearing the path towards your success.

I attract positivity and positive people in my life

Our company tends to define us. Like our mothers used to say, your company can make or break your character. And if we are surrounded by positive people, positivity will become a part of your life. And success will follow suit.

I grow with every challenge I face

Challenges makes you stronger in your pursuit towards success. And you have to remember that you grow with every trial and tribulation. So, keep telling yourself that I am growing stronger with every problem I face and solve.

I will surely succeed

Yes, this is the most important mantra that you need to engrave on your mind. Keep telling yourself that you are born to succeed and no amount of hardships and problems can stop you from succeeding.

Always remember, failure is not your enemy. Instead, it tells you where you went wrong in your plan of action and how you can rectify it. Don't run away from failures. Embrace them, accept them, and finally use them to create a better master plan to reach the destination that awaits you.

> *"Life is what we make it, always has been, always will be."*
> *-Grandma Moses*

Part 2

Success Blueprint

S P Garg

After enjoying wonderful reading of life and success chapters of Part 1, the readers would be delighted to go through the following chapters, which will be shedding some light on the remarkable journeys of some great people, highlighting their failures, struggles and then finally success. The chapter is titled "Ordinary people: Extra ordinary Success".

Next two chapters are the blueprints/action plan for entrepreneurs, startups, managers, professionals, and others for achieving success in every walk of life in this competitive global scenario.

Finally, what matters in life: only happiness. And that is the main purpose of this book.

Chapter 12

Ordinary People: Extraordinary Success
(Learnings from success stories)

We should all know how to handle failure. Managing failure is the biggest management lesson that one should learn during their lifetime. Young people should understand how to manage failure because you have to consider yourself as the project chief of the problems. Therefore, you should become the captain of the problem and defeat the problem and succeed.

Learning uses creativity, creativity leads to thinking and knowledge makes you great. History proves that who dare to imagine the impossible are the ones who break human limitations. In every field of human endeavor whether science, medicine anything, you must break the limitations.

To promote learning about and learning from real-life examples of pure grit and purposefulness, this chapter includes a myriad of motivational stories from the lives of people under the headings of **"Ordinary People, Extraordinary Lives"** so that readers get inspired.(randomly selected)

APJ Abdul Kalam: Inspiration to millions

(In the science and technology field, failure is the stepping stone to success. Kalam was a good scientist- cum- good human)

Dr. APJ Abdul Kalam resides in the heart of every Indian. He is popularly known as the "Missile man of India" and

"People's President". He was a great scientist who made many inventions. Born to a boatman Tamil family in Rameshwaram, Kalam even struggled to bring bread and butter to the house. As a result, he started working at an early age to reduce the financial burdens and problems.

But the best part was that his father nurtured him in a spiritual environment that influenced his lifestyle. He developed a keen interest in studies and he was inquisitive to learn new things. Throughout his life, he kept learning and imparting knowledge. He maintained the same enthusiasm of learning each passing second.

Despite these hardships, Kalam managed to complete his higher studies at St. Joseph College, Tiruchirapalli in aeronautical engineering at the Madras Institute of Technology(MIT).

After this, he gave an interview at DTDP and IAF to be a fighter pilot. But he could receive a call from the Directorate of Technical Development and Production (DTDP) only. He even failed the test by a whisker in the Indian Air force (IAF) by just one rank. He then decided to never look back. He kept working hard at DTDP. He kept experimenting, some failed, some worked but he never gave up. He worked hard from the Pokhran-II nuclear test in 1998 to rising so high that he headed up India's Missile program.

Success

Finally, he performed excellently in his job over the passing years and got promoted as the senior scientific assistant. During this time, he acted as a primary human resource in the development of India's first indigenous satellite launch vehicle

(SLV-III). His projects such as Light Combat Aircraft were a huge success.

As a result, he served as a Chief Economic Advisor to the Prime Minister and the secretary of DRDO (Defence Research and Development Organisation) from July 1992 to December 1999.

He was awarded the civilian awards- Padma Bhushan in 1981, Padma Vibhushan in 1990, and the highest Civilian award in 1997.

In 2011, he launched his mission **"What Can I give"** under which he was appointed as Chancellor of IIST (Indian Institute of Space, Science, and Technology), a guest faculty at IIM Ahmedabad, IIT Indore, and many more institutes across India.

Then he also received honorary doctorate degrees from over 40 renowned universities and institutes. During his life journey, he worked on 4 books named "Wings of fire", "My Journey", "India 2020- a vision for the new Millenium" and "Ignited mind- unleashing the power within India" in multiple languages.

He died on 27th July 2015 at IIM Shillong while delivering a lecture when he suffered a heart attack.

Lessons Learned

Dream before your dreams can come true as dreams transform into thoughts and thoughts result in action.

Keep yourself motivated enough to accept failure if it is a reality that cannot be changed.

To succeed in your mission, you must have single-minded devotion to your goal.

Nelson Mandela: Your life-vision reflects hope to stay consistent in any situation

(Nelson Mandela was an Anti-apartheid revolutionary, a statesman, and a philanthropist)

Nelson fought against white and black discrimination to live together in harmony with equal opportunity. He cherished the idea of a free and democratic society such that it was a feeling for his survival and living. He won some social fights and some lost also, but still, he is admired for his values

Failures

> Mandela was just 12 years old when he lost his father, which changed his life badly. Immediately he left his village to take classes in African history, English, Geography, etc. He performed well in studies despite all the challenges. But, being a black man, he had only one option to enroll in special schools for blacks in South Africa for higher studies.
>
> With this, he struggled to bring dollars home and worked as a guard and clerk while completing his bachelor's degree. Even after so much happening, he never compromised on his studies. After all this, he pursued and enrolled himself in a law course later in the University of Witwatersrand in Johannesburg.
>
> The law course encouraged him to stand against the racial discrimination, he had to face during his early age. He made the agenda of his life to protest against discrimination. Therefore, he joined the African National Congress (ANC) in his mid-twenties to lead multiple campaigns against racism. This was just one example,

where he was the main part of the Civil Disobedience movement in his nation.

Due to regular protests, his party ANC was banned in 1961. Then he founded his military wing "**Umkhonto we Sizwe**" and led underground guerilla attacks against state institutions. While all this, he had the greatest challenge to arrange funds for his party. Without any further thinking, he himself eloped to a foreign country to manage financial support for his army. He was welcomed back with a life imprisonment for 27 years by the US govt.

But, during these 27 years also, he used to deliver his message of social equality whenever he got the chance. He never left a chance to mesmerize and influence his people with his powerful words. This gave him a stage and audience and a chance to become a public figure.

Success

We all know, he created history as he was awarded the Nobel Peace Prize in 1993. He was an inspiration to all those, who wish to take revenge. Even though he was locked up in jail for 27 years, he still prayed for the peace of the person who imprisoned him.

After this, he was nominated as the first black head of state in a fully representative democratic election, a South African president from 1994-1999. During this time, he served the people as a servant and not as a Prophet.

He lived a long successful life as a Hero even at 100, contributing to many social causes like helping children and HIV-AIDS patients.

Spreading all this happiness among the natives, he died on Dec 5, 2013. He remains a challenge and competitor for the current politicians in the nation. He is an inspiration to many young talents.

Lessons Learned

> Life is not about only colors, you need to stand and fight with what you believe. Standing for oneself is quite easier than standing for the rights of the nation.
>
> Never let anyone plan and control your destiny because you are greater than you look. What makes decisions better for a person. It is "you", who stands against all adversity boldly.
>
> Success is determined by learning and knowledge. Things will come and go, but the everlasting thing is your education.

Abraham Lincoln: Successful people maintain Emotional Quotient over Intelligence Quotient

(Lincoln was the 16th President of the United States of America)

Lincoln was born into poverty in a log cabin raised in Indiana. Was self-educated. Studied law. Abraham Lincoln, sixteenth President of the United States, was born near Hodgenville, Kentucky on February 12, 1809. His family moved to Indiana when he was seven, and he grew up on the edge of the frontier. He had very little formal education, but read voraciously when not working on his father's farm.

As a young man, he joined the military service as a Blachoc wars captain, but later he left that. With a very formal education, Lincon taught himself and became a Lawyer and Congressmen himself.

His real rise to national prominence could also be viewed as a "failure".

In 1832, he lost his job and lost in the state legislature elections. In 1833, Lincoln failed in his business. Still, he stood again in Illinois state elections and managed to win it. This success was not ever-lasting for him.

In 1835, he lost his better half to destiny. All these consecutive downfalls broke down his nervous system. But again, he won the state elections and even received the license to practice law in state courts and became a law partner of John T. Stuart.

He was nominated by the Whig Caucus for Illinois House Speaker. But he was defeated in the elections. He was defeated for nomination for congress in 1843.

But, after a struggle of 3 years, he was elected to congress. He chose not to run for congress in 1848, abiding by the rule of rotation among Whigs. In 1849, he was rejected as a land officer. Then got rejected even against the US Senate. But finally, he was elected as the president of the nation.

In his repeated failures, he would remind himself to make sure to put his feet(efforts) in the right place and then stand firm. If Lincoln had quit at the time when the going had been tough for all the world, then the world would have been a different place.

Success

He became a Whig Party leader and Illinois State legislator. In 1849, he returned to practicing law but was vexed by the opening of additional lands to slavery as a result of the Kansas-Nebraska Act.

In 1858, he entered politics, tried for a seat in the Illinois senate. This led to a series of highly contested debates known as the Lincoln on Douglas Debate. Lincoln lost the elections but impressed a lot of people with his loss. So, he kept up the politics ahead.

Two years later, he ran for president and won. He became the leader of the new Republican Party which reached a national audience in the 1854 debate against Stephen Douglas.

In 1861, he became president of the US. He led the nation through civil war, against , cultural, constitutional, and political crises. He also took part in modernizing the US economy. He was considered one of the best presidents in the United States of America's history.

He was assassinated in 1865 and he was no more.

Lessons learned

Do whatever it takes to become the leader of change.

Develop an ability to retain emotional balance in difficult times by self-awareness.

Try dispelling your anxiety in constructive ways.

Shri Lal Bahadur Shastri: Lead with Spirits

(The 2nd Prime Minister of India)

Struggles

Shri Lal Bahadur Shastri was born in 1904 at Mughalsarai in Uttar Pradesh. His father was a school teacher who died when he was only a year and a half old. His mother took care of him along with her other three children. His childhood pet name was "Nanhe."

His small-town schooling was not remarkable in any way, but he had a happy enough childhood despite the poverty that bogged him. He was sent to live with an uncle in Varanasi to high school. He used to walk many miles to school without shoes, even when the streets burned under summer's heat.

As he grew up, Lal Bahadur Shastri became more and more interested in the country's struggle for freedom from Britishers. He was greatly impressed by Mahatma Gandhi's struggle for the nation. Following Gandhi's ideology, he joined the Non-Cooperation Movement when he was only sixteen. The Institution Vidya Peeth awarded Shastri the bachelor's degree in Varanasi. In 1927, he got married with Lalita Devi. In 1930, he dedicated his life to the freedom struggle. He led many defiant campaigns and spent seven years in British jails.

Success

When the Congress Government was formed in 1946, Shastri was called upon to play a constructive role in the country's governance. Accordingly, he was appointed Parliamentary Secretary in his home state of Uttar Pradesh and soon rose to the position of Home Minister.

His capacity for hard work and his efficiency became a byword in Uttar Pradesh. He moved to New Delhi in 1951 and held several portfolios in the Union Cabinet – Minister for Railways; Minister for Transport and Communications; Minister for Commerce and Industry; Home Minister; and during Nehru's illness Minister without portfolio. He resigned his post as Minister for Railways because he felt responsible for a railway accident in which many lives were lost. Parliament and the country greatly appreciated the unprecedented gesture.

In between his Ministerial assignments, the Congress Party succeeded in the General Elections of 1952, 1957, and 1962. This 'Little dynamo of a man' served his nation dedicatedly for more than thirty years with great integrity and competence. He was humble and tolerant, with great inner strength. He was a man who understood the people's language and led his nation towards progress. He died in Uzbekistan in 1996.

Lessons Learned

Discipline And Combined Action Brings Real Strength to A Nation.

Loyalty Is the Key to Anything, And One Should Not Compromise It for What He Receives.

Strength And Power Lie in Unity. A Leader Takes All His Companions Together in Any Fight.

Lady Gaga: Never be afraid to create and start

(A famous American musician and actress)

Lady Gaga is regarded as a best-selling artist. She has continuously maintained "pop culture". Hence, she was nick-named the name "Lady Gaga" by one of the producers. Her music has been one of the best journeys that many musicians live to admire. She has outsmarted the music world and her songs are highly recommended. She lives to be an American Idol forever

Struggles

Lady Gaga's full name is Stefani Joanne Angelina Germanotta. She was born in 1986 in New York. Her mother enrolled her in piano classes and creative arts camp. While she was a young girl, she showed a lot of interest in music. She proceeded to grow her talents and when she was a young teenager, she played music at open mic nights and different gigs at their place.

Her childhood was a misfit as she was mocked severally for being either too proactive or too eccentric. She was even raped when she was just 14 years of age, which led her to fall in a psychological torture as she was dumped by her parents at that hard time. She did not lose her courage and graduated in acting.

She then wanted to start and build a career for herself. She auditioned for New York Shows but did not qualify. She decided to get out of acting and pursue her love for music. She then enrolled in a music school.

Success

Her debut songs were rated the top in the US Billboard 200. Her second album sold over one million copies and one million downloads in the first week becoming the best song sold on iTunes Store.

She won many awards in her acting role including Best Actress in the Golden Globe Award, an Academy Grammy, BAFTA, and Golden Globe Award.

By the year 2014, Lady Gaga sold over 124 million records. Lady Gaga and her team have supported some of the known artists who have managed to become celebrities in no time.

They include Nicki Minaj, Milley Cirus, Halsey, Sam Smith, Cardi B just to mention a few.

Lady Gaga even worked as a songwriter for Sony and signed a contract with Interscope Records and Akon's label. She has also ventured into the beauty world where she managed to open an account with Amazon in September 2019 that deals with makeup accessories going by the name Haus Laboratories which emerged number one as the best lipstick brand.

She was given the platform of singing the US National Anthem during the inauguration of the 46th President Joe Biden which was such an honor for her.

Lesson Learned

Life is slow but work-in-progress. Live easy and work hard.

You won't be happy until you accept yourself.

You do not need to show yourself as a victim. Nobody can help you more than yourself.

Oprah Winfrey: Turn Your Wounds into Wisdom

(African- American Television producer, actress, author, and philanthropist)

Struggles

Oprah's childhood was filled with abuse that no one should experience. Winfrey was born in 1954 as an illegitimate child. For the first 6 years of her life, Winfrey was raised by her strict grandmother in poverty. At age 3, her grandmother taught her to read and excel in school. She won a scholarship at high school.

They were so poor that even her dress was made of potato sacks. Her grandmother used to whip her so badly that she had wounds on all her back.

From age 9 to 13, she was sexually abused by her cousin, uncle, and a family friend. At 14, Winfrey became pregnant, but the baby was born premature and died.

Yet against all the odds, she became a Co-Anchor on a Radio show at 19. Then, she went on to have the highest Hero 14 rated T.V. show in that category. A show that was syndicated for straight 25 years.

She was the wealthiest African-American of the 20th century and America's first Black Multi-Billionaire. She is a Hero and role model to all those who battle oppression and adversity and is one of the most prominent philanthropists of our times.

Then Oprah moved away to live with her father in Tennessee, where she attended Tennessee State University and got her start in communications. During high school, Winfrey got a part-time job at a local black radio station. She attended East Nashville High School, where she became a member of the drama club, the national Forensics league, and the honor society.

She also represented his school at the White House conference. Her first debut started as an anchor at radio station WVOL to read weekly news. She wins the contest for Miss Fire Prevention. From there, she grew up writing a journal for herself.

At 19, she began co-anchoring the local evening news. Due to her efforts, she got selected as the first black Tennessee. At that time, she was both the youngest news anchor and the first black female news anchor for Nashville's WLAC-TV. She dropped out of college and went for a job in Baltimore.

Baltimore offered many opportunities to her destiny. Her meeting with production assistant Gayle King was one of the best things that happened to her. They both became close friends to each other.

Success

In 1983, Oprah Winfrey's big break came, and she started hosting Chicago's low-rated half-hour morning talk show, AM Chicago. Then Oprah met her significant half, Stedman Graham.

Within months, the show became the first highest-rated Talk show hosted by a woman in Chicago. 3 years later, her show was expanded to a full hour show, renamed The Oprah Winfrey Show, and went national making Winfrey a Millionaire. It was then purchased by the King brother's corporation.

She also found her own company named Harpo Productions. She was presented with the National Organization for Women Achievement Award. Her role of Sofia in the color paper was nominated for an academy award.

Winfrey is a perfect example of what is possible regardless of where you were born and how you were raised.

Lessons learned

You get in life what you have the courage to ask for.

The great courage one must do is to step out of our past and history. So that we can dream and achieve big things.

Avoid negative people and thoughts from your life and focus on attracting positive energy.

Jack Ma: Whatever it takes, try it again
(Founder of the Alibaba Group Collection)

Jack Ma is a business tycoon from China who has been worldly known for his great donation towards the Covid-19 pandemic.

Struggles

Jack Ma was born in China in 1964. His real name being Hangzhou Zhejiang and was given the name Jack by tourist friends who found it hard to pronounce his name. Jack worked on taking tourists on tours at the Hangzhou International Hotel so that he could learn how to speak English.

Jack failed his college entrance exams three times and he felt discouraged. He was failing mainly in the mathematics paper. But he finally enrolled and graduated with a Bachelor of Arts in English at the Teachers Institute.

Jack then applied to Harvard School ten times and was always rejected. But that did not stop him from pushing harder. He worked as a lecturer for some time. His life was never easy while growing up. He was rejected multiple times for his 30 jobs.

Jack then with his friend, a computer teacher, created a website named Hangzhou Haibo Translation Agency which gained him some major investment clients. The company made a lot of profit within the shortest time possible.

He then started working on building websites for big companies. After a while, Jack returned to Hangzhou with his work colleagues and created Alibaba while in his apartment. The platform offered online business marketing. The company grew to be a great success winning awards from all over the world.

Success

Alibaba won the amazing title of the world's largest initial public offering in a US financial report. He was selected as a young global leader in his career. He opened many parallel sites including Taobao Marketplace, Alipay, Lynx, Ali mama, etc to improve the e-commerce system in their country. He also invested in Yahoo company with $1 billion.

He was named in the top ten economic personalities of the year. He was also selected by Fortune as the 25 most powerful businessperson in Asia among many other awards he received in his life. He is known for his charitable donations of masks and vaccines to major affected countries of the covid-19 pandemic.

Lesson learned

    Never complain in life. Always make sure that you keep the struggle alive and go for whatever you want the moment you want it and you shall possess.

    Do not take things too seriously. Keep enjoying your life. The objective of life is to make it a fun

    Never give up. If you fail to accomplish your goal but see the process till the end, then you are a success.

Mira Chanu: Add on more strength and more power even if it is 1kg

(Olympics winner weightlifter)

She is an Indian weightlifter who has become a great inspiration to many girls who think sporting activities are only achieved by men. It is often said that the going is tough, but the fruits are sweet. Mira Chanu is now a walking image of any woman who appreciates sports in life.

Struggles

Mirabai Chanu was born in 1994 in Manipur, India. Mirabai's father Saikhom Kriti Singh's income from his job as a construction worker in the Manipur Public Works Department wasn't enough. Her mother would run a small tea kiosk on the village main road to support the family.

In order to maintain her weight, Mirabai used to skip meals at times. She even could not attend her sister's wedding because of the competition.

When she was 12 years, Saikhom Mirabai Chanu could easily carry a huge bundle of firewood more than her older brother. She began practicing in 2007 and used to travel 20 km daily for practice. At the age of 11, she became the Under-15 champion and at the age of 17, she became the Junior champion.

She won her first breakthrough at the Glasgow edition of the Commonwealth. She has had many failures in her life including the scenario where she failed to finish in the women's 48kg in the 2016 Rio Olympics. She had no successful lifts in any of her 3 attempts on the clean and jerk section. This made her feel afraid and continued working on sharpening her skills.

During 2017, she managed to win the Gold medal in the women's 48kg category lifting a competition record 194 kg in total in the 2017 World Weightlifting Championships.

In 2019, she lifted a total of 201kgs emerging 4th and a personal level best in the 49kg weightlifting. Working hard through her moves, she later improved and lifted 203kgs in the 49kgs Senior National Weightlifting Championships winning her the gold medal.

Women discrimination has been highly ranked in the Indian culture but this never limited Chanu to be the best in what she loves doing.

Success

Mira Chanu has won many awards including the silver medal at the 2020 Summer Olympics in Women's 48kg, the Padma Shri and the Major Dhyan Chand Khel Ratna Award where she was also given national rewards and recommendations. Chanu brought female gender sports into glory and encouraged them to take part in sporting activities all over India.

Lesson learned

Quitters are never winners.

Always strive to excel in every situation every day of your life and you will win the prizes at the end of it all.

Richard Branson: Persistence personifies

(An English business tycoon and philanthropist who owns the Virgin Group)

Struggles

Richard Branson was born as Richard Charles Nicholas Branson in 1950 in Surrey, England to Edward James Branson and Eve Branson.

Branson always had the entrepreneurial streak in him and a knack for making money. He could eye an opportunity where there was none and make it into a successful business.

As a child, he did not perform well in school. Because of his dyslexia, Branson was always struggling to keep up in school. He went from Scaitcliffe School to the Stowe School, a boarding school in Buckinghamshire, England.

At 16, he decided to drop out for good. This socially unconventional move led him to write a youth-culture magazine for students.

This led to the birth of Virgin, a mail-order company that provided his magazine's funding. Virgin Records bands were catapulted among the top record companies worldwide.

Soon, the financial struggles added up by 1992. The next year, Branson had to sell it to THORN EMI for $1 billion. Prior to this setback, Branson added two travel companies under his belt: the Voyager Group and Virgin Atlantic.

His first store in Oxford Street eventually multiplied into a series of Virgin megastores. In the same year of the sale, he opened Virgin Radio. Apart from having to sell Virgin Records,

Branson also suffered from other business failures such as Virgin Cola, Virgin Cosmetics, and Virgin Brides.

Then he started again, and bloomed. From Music to Media, Finance, Outer Space and Everything in-between

Branson diversified his businesses and added an airline, Virgin Atlantic, in 1984. He leased his first 747 to fly from New York to Gatwick, making Virgin Atlantic compete against British Airways.

Success

His other big firms include Virgin Media, Virgin Money, and even Virgin Trains. All his companies fall under the Virgin Group, which includes more than 200 companies spread throughout the world. Branson has gone a long way from simply opening up a business to fund another.

The Spaceship Company is a Virgin Galactic company that Branson established so he could continue his dream of exploring space and bringing that experience to more individuals.

This business exemplifies Branson's ability to move on despite past failures. In 2014, the first test flight destroyed the original ship. But this year, Virgin Galactic's SpaceShipTwo (SS2) successfully made its first test flight of the craft's atmospheric re-entry system.

Virgin promised that SS2 could accommodate six passengers and two pilots. The spaceship's size would also provide the out-of-seat zero-gravity experience and large windows to see the rest of the view.

Branson is looking further into the future with his latest investment in Hyperloop One, a company building high-speed transport and cargo pods that move at 250 miles per hour.

The Philanthropist in Him believes in giving back to society. He started his first charity when he was just 17.

Whenever Virgin Galactic is likely to send non-astronauts into space. And today, at the age of 67, he is going strong and continues to expand his more than fifty-year-old legacy.

Lessons learned

Find happiness in small and little things. Enjoy every day of your life.

Define your own instead of copying other people path

Acquiring skills and talent is equally and more important than just acquiring formal education.

Martin Luther King Jr: A spokesperson of equality and perseverance

Failures from early childhood

Martin Luther King Jr. Was given to him by his father, who attended many religious outreaches worldwide. His father being a general overseer, Martin and his siblings were involved in religion, and reading the Bible every day was a norm.

Being enrolled in a black school and not being friends with white people, King was oppressed. He was tempted to hate all the white people, but his religious teachings were against hating anyone, which his mother never became reluctant to remind him.

King later enrolled himself in an African-American school where he maintained high scores. After that, he became the manager of a newspaper delivery station in Atlanta. While in high school, King developed a knack for public speaking and consistently took part in it. He specialized in English and Sociology. In addition, he was into fashion design wherein he wore patent leather shoes and tweed suits, gaining home the nickname "Tweed / Tweedie."

He went through college and paid for his tuition fees by picking up tobacco. Later on, King led a bus boycott against the oppression of the black people. The boycott lasted for almost a year, and King was arrested and became a hot topic nationally, consistently featuring in the news, increasing his public reputation.

King was arrested several times, gaining respect and admiration for his grit and determination towards the fruition of his cause. Finally, during the 1963 campaigns, King was arrested, and this was when he composed the most important historical document, "The Letter from Birmingham Jail," calling for social changes in society.

In this manuscript of a multi-volume edition, he laid out his plans, dreams, and thoughts for America's future. This book also included the need for better jobs, higher payment wages, decent and reliable housing, and good quality education for all people.

In 1967, Dr. Martin Luther King, Jr. separated himself from the needs of the civil rights movement. He went ahead and rented a house in Jamaica with no telephone signals and labored over his final manuscript, which was unavailable for ten years. King faced a near-death incident when he went to the signing of his book ceremony.

Success

King had been received numerous awards during his lifetime. These included 50 honorary degrees from various universities. In addition, he was the youngest winner of the Nobel Peace Prize, the American Liberties Medal, Spingarn Medal, Margaret Sanger Award, a three-time nominee for the Grammy Awards, and more.

Lessons Learned

> Never be afraid to fight for what you believe is right. Never be condemned by your color, race, or religion. It is time to rise above all this.
>
> Freedom is never voluntarily given by the oppressor(boss); it must be demanded by the oppressed(submissive/employee),
>
> Be resilient persistent in your actions.

Walt Disney: Reality Lies In The Dreamland

(An American entrepreneur, a film producer, an actor-writer, and an animator)

Walt Disney is regarded as the King of animations, a true cultural icon. He is universally appreciated and recognized as the harbinger of cartoon media. His tiny palace, created as a dream, has grown to be an admired attraction worldwide. As a result, Disney World Parks have grown in size and attracted tourists worldwide.

Life Experience

Born in Chicago in 1901 and raised in Missouri, Disney was the fourth son among five siblings. Disney had a strained relationship with Elias, an authoritarian figure, allegedly abusive and non-earning.

To escape from his stressful circumstances, the youngster found comfort in drawing, and to earn some income, he decided to join the US Army, wherein he was rejected due to his age. Finally, after a lot of struggle, he settled for a decent job, albeit drawing cartoons during this time. He grew better and better at his artwork with time.

His first venture, Laugh-O-Gram Studios, in 1920, went bankrupt which was launched by him and his older brother Roy. With the loss of his first business, Disney packed his bags, and with just $40 to his name, took off to Los Angeles to try his hand at acting. But he failed at that, too. Still, there was a silver lining. Noticing there weren't any animation studios in California, Disney convinced Roy to join him.

Not so long after, Disney found its first significant success with the creation of Oswald the Lucky Rabbit. Traveling to New York to renegotiate his contract, he discovered that his producer had taken his team of animators from him and that he no longer had any legal rights to them. But instead of fighting the loss, Disney decided to walk away and start over again. So on the train ride back to California, he created Mickey Mouse in 1928.

Disney had a nervous breakdown after creating Mickey Mouse as the bankers rejected the concept of his famous mouse over 300 times before finding success. Then, during World War II, the animators went on strike and contributed to his mounting debt that ran upwards of $4 million. Finally, the opening of Disneyland was called 'Black Sunday' as Forged tickets were bringing more visitors than anticipated.

Success

His venture grew so big within a short period that he opened another branch of Disneyland in Anaheim, California. Kids loved his work, so they wished to see all the animations he created and the place he lived. This brought him to his life success.

In 1937 he created Snow White and the Seven Dwarfs, Pinocchio and Fantasia (both 1940), and Bambi (1942). He also produced movies like Mickey Mouse(1928), snow-white(1937), Cinderella(1950), and many others. Walt Disney is a 22 time Oscar winner from 59 nominations. In addition, he is a 2-time Golden Globe Special Achievement winner and an Emmy Award winner. These are just some mentions of his many achievements.

Walt Disney passed away in 1996, leaving behind a legacy that will always be cherished.

Lessons Learned

> If you can dream it, you can do it. Life is too short to settle for possible things. Learn to pursue the impossible; seek what others cannot be done.
>
> The way to get started is to quit talking and begin doing.
>
> You can design and create the most beautiful things in the world. But it takes time and effort to turn your imagination into reality.

Maya Angelou: We Have the Power Within Us To Win Against The Storm

(Marguerite Annie Johnson is known as a memoirist, poet, and civil rights activist, writer of plays, movies, and TV shows)

Maya Angelou was born in St. Louis, Missouri, in 1928. "Maya" was a nickname given by her older brother, who loved calling her "Maya Sister. "Following her parent's marriage breaking up, Angelou and her brother went and lived with their grandmother for a while. Unfortunately, their biological father left them, and their mother started dating a man called Freeman. This man forcibly took advantage of Angelou's innocence and raped her.

He was arrested for a day and was mysteriously murdered after four days. Angelou felt so guilty about his death that she didn't talk for almost five years. She believed that her voice had killed the man. Angelou went into depression for a while. This isolated her and left her engrossed in deep thoughts. She developed a passion for literature reading and developed her listening skills and observation.

She later enrolled in school, where she met her favourite teacher, who introduced her to the art of poetry. Before she finished school, Angelou started working as a streetcar conductor in San Francisco. She used to tell her mother that this was her dream job.

Her mother greatly admired Angelou's efforts. Then she became a mother herself and gave birth to a son at 17 years.

She joined dance classes to lose weight with her friends. Unfortunately, she performed below average to the extent that she failed in all the contested finals.

But this dancing skill helped her earn an extra income to support her son as she started dancing in nightclubs. Her dance performance style was known as "calypso," making her popular among the people.

Success

This enabled her to record her first album, Miss Calypso. The album took her to Broadway, where she performed her Calypso Heat Wave film compositions. After that, she became famous, left her dancing job, and started writing. She also joined an activism group cheering for Fidel Castro and later for Obama.

Angelou lost so many important people in her life that it pushed her against the walls. But her desire to rise and work towards her goal made her strong. She later met with Malcolm X in Ghana, subsequently assassinated. Angelou returned home and joined Martin Lurther King Jr. In his pursuit, who was later assassinated.

She fell into a deep depression and decided to write a ten-part series called "Black, Blues, Black!" which focused on Africanism.

She was later internationally celebrated and recognized when she wrote her first autobiography, "I Know Why The Caged Bird Sings."

Since then, she has published many books in her life and taken part in theatre activities. She later became a teacher and professor in her hometown. She was accredited with many awards and recognitions, including more than thirty honorary degrees from all over the world.

Angelou became a mentor and friend to Oprah Winfrey. She once recited one of her poems during Bill Clinton's inauguration, winning a Grammy Award. Her second poem was repeated during the 50th anniversary of the United Nations.

Lessons learned.

Caring for someone is akin to success.

If you do not like something, strive to change it. If you're unable to, change your attitude.

A wise person refuses to be a victim of anyone and does not victimize anyone at any cost.

Abraham Lincoln: Successful people Maintain Emotional Quotient Over Intelligence Quotient

(Lincoln is the 16th President of the United States of America)

Abraham Lincoln, the sixteenth President of the United States, was born near Hodgenville, Kentucky, on February 12, 1809. His family moved to Indiana when he was seven, and he grew up on the frontier's edge. He had very little formal education but read voraciously when not working on his father's farm.

As a young man, he joined military service during the Black Hawk Wars and was elected Captain of his first company, although luckily never experienced combat during his tenure. With very little formal education, Lincoln later pursued further studies and became a Lawyer and Congressman through his own will.

His natural rise to national prominence could also be viewed as a "failure."

In 1832, he lost his job and also lost in the state legislature elections. In 1833, Lincoln failed in his business. Still, he stood again in Illinois state elections and managed to win it. Unfortunately, this success was not lasting.

In 1835, he lost his better half. All these consecutive downfalls broke down his nervous system. But again, he won the state elections and even received the license to practice law in state courts and became John T. Stuart's law partner.

The Whig Caucus nominated him for Illinois House Speaker. But he was defeated in the elections and at the nomination for congress in 1843.

But, after a struggle of 3 years, he was elected. He chose not to run for congress in 1848, abiding by the rule of rotation among Whigs. In 1849, he was further rejected as a land officer. Then got left even against the US Senate. But finally, he was elected as the President of the nation.

In his repeated failures, he would remind himself to make sure to put his feet (efforts) in the right place and then stand firm. If Lincoln had quit when the going had been burdensome, then the world would have been a different place.

Success

He became a Whig Party leader and Illinois State legislator. In 1849, he returned to practicing law but was vexed by opening additional lands to slavery due to the Kansas-Nebraska Act.

In 1858, he entered politics tried for a seat in the Illinois senate. This led to highly contested debates known as the Lincoln on Douglas Debate. Lincoln lost the elections but impressed a lot of people with his loss.

Two years later, he ran for President and won. He became the leader of the new Republican Party, which reached a national audience in the 1854 debate against Stephen Douglas.

In 1861, he became President of the US. He led the nation through a civil war against cultural, constitutional, and political crises. He also took part in the modernization of the US economy. He was considered one of the best presidents in the United States of America's history.

He was assassinated in 1865.

Lessons Learned

>Sometimes one must persist in sheer faith and will to achieve their heart's desires, even in the face of consistent failure and agony.
>
>Develop an ability to retain emotional balance in difficult times by self-awareness.
>
>Try dispelling your anxiety in constructive ways.

Amitabh Bachchan: Life is a movie, and we decide on how we want to act it

(A Hollywood actor, film producer, TV host, occasional playback singer, brand endorsements, and former politician)

Amitabh is a prime example of someone being pegged back repeatedly in life, personally and professionally. Yet he fought back successfully. He is a perfect role model not only for the ones who want to become movie stars. But also for the rest of the world.

Vintage King and the Sher shah of Bollywood was born in 1942 in Allahabad to the Hindi poet Harivansh Rai Bachchan and his wife, the social activist Teji Bachchan. He was educated at Sherwood College, Nainital, and Kirori Mal College, University of Delhi.

Failures

After the completion of higher education, his father approached the founder of Prithvi Theater (Prithviraj Kapoor) to see if he would give his son a job, but Bachchan was rejected. He then applied for a role as a newsreader for a radio company but failed the audition.

He decided to become a business executive for a company in Kolkata and then started working in theater before starting his film career.

The early struggles started with working as a theater artist. Then a broadcaster AIR rejected Amitabh Bachan for his deep voice. He had no house to live and was thus offered a rented apartment by Mr. Mehmood, a comedian.

He also worked as a voice narrator in 1969 in an award-winning film. Then he was offered an acting role as one of the 7 protagonists in the Saat Hindustani film. This opened doors for him to the film industry with many super hits.

But again, he was declared bankrupt during the early 20th century when his venture Amitabh Bachchan Corporation Limited faced failure of the production, distribution, and event Management Company.

He again made a comeback with the help of actor-cum-producer Yash Raj Chopra. After this, he left no chance to impress his audiences and was awarded with Padma Shri, the 4th highest Civilian Honor of India in 1984, Padma Bhushan, the 3rd highest Civilian Honor of India in 2001, and Padma Vibhushan, 2nd highest Civilian Award in 2015.

Not only the Indian government, but other countries also awarded him with honorary citizenship including France.

He lives a luxurious life that many people dream of living. From house to cars, he has everything, top class. He is on the top numbers in the list of the "Highest-paid celebrities".

Lessons Learned

Life is a movie, and we decide on how we want to act it.

Go for what you want and stop at no cost working towards it.

Success comes slowly. One needs to be patient while doing anything.

Stephen Edwin King: Think, reason, and make it a success

(America's most exemplary author of fantasy novels, fiction, horror, supernatural, crime, science-fiction, and suspense books)

Struggles

Stephen King was born in 1947 in Portland and attended Durham Elementary School. King was interested in writing from a very young age. At school, he used to contribute articles to the school magazine.

He grew up with a single mother and an older brother, and they underwent a lot of financial crises. Their father died, which forced them to live at their relative's places. He struggled to manage funds for his education.

His journey towards becoming a celebrated author began when he was a teenager. He used to write stories in college, where he stored many of them in a crate under his bed, not knowing he was better than he imagined. Writing them gave him a chance to earn an extra income before he got a job. This also gave him a platform to create and blend his styles in writing. As a result, he became better at what he did with time.

After a while, he got a job and worked as a school teacher, and that was when he changed his writing style and started writing novels. He wrote his first novel called "Carrie," which got rejected 30 times. He did not have the heart to take it, so he gave up and threw his manuscript in a trash bin.

But later on, his wife encouraged him not to despair and try for the last time. Stephen considered this and went ahead and tried his luck. The time was the charm, and the manuscript was accepted. The book was published later. Carrie gave King the exposure that he needed. The book was sold all over the world, and this gave him success in the horror genre.

Success

He was now known as the "Horror King" because of the many novels, including Salem Lot, The Shining, The Stand, and many more. Some of his books have been turned into big-budget Hollywood films performed by the greatest. He has won many awards, including the British Fantasy awards, Grand Master Award, and the National Medal of Arts.

He has written over 200 short stories and 350 million copies of books, and he has published 63 novels under his pen name "Richard Bachman".

Lessons learned

> Keep persevering in your mission to succeed. Multiply your efforts and do better than the previous version of yourself.

Practice enough that it brushes up your skills for improvement and not for perfection.

Welcome interruptions and distractions. Do not let them take a toll on your career and success.

Vincent Wlliam Van Gogh: Accept Your Differences to Turn Them Into Opportunities.

(Regarded As the Greatest Artist of His Time and After)

He was born in 1853 in the Netherlands to a minister. He became passionate about his skills from a very young age. He used watercolors mostly while in school. He was a very quiet and nature-loving kid.

Van Gogh started working at age 16 when his uncle got him a job as a trainee with an art dealership in The Hague. He went on to do stints in the firm's London and Paris offices before he was fired in 1876.

Afterward, he worked briefly as a schoolteacher in England then at a bookstore back in the Netherlands. Then, in 1878, he went to the Borinage, a mining district in Belgium, and worked among the poor as a lay preacher.

When his attempt to become a preacher didn't work out, he sketched out local miners and peasants while living in Belgium and decided in 1880 to focus on art. In 1881, his younger brother Theo, an art dealer, helped support him financially and emotionally.

In 1886, Van Gogh went to live with Theo in Paris, and his two years in the French capital proved pivotal. He was exposed to the work of Impressionist and Neo-Impressionist artists and started using a lighter, brighter palette and experimenting with brushstroke techniques.

He was tempted several times by his immediate family, an uncle, who owned a gallery, and asked Vincent for a picture of the Hague so that he could rate his work. Still, he disapproved, saying it did not meet his expectations.

But this did not stop Vincent from continuing doing what he loved most. He did not give up. He persevered and continued adding more energy to his artwork. He gained a lot of criticism because most of his artwork was mainly black and white.

He moved to London later. He started experiencing depression while living in Belgium because of his Protestant Religion. He became sick and lonely, with no money to support himself, so he moved back to his parent's home.

He spent his last two years in the south of France, where he produced a number of his best-known paintings. By his death in 1890, van Gogh had started to garner critical acclaim. He created some of his most famous paintings while in a mental asylum.

He sold just a handful of about 850 paintings and nearly 1,300 works on paper during his decade-long career.

He started creating landscapes and still life that grew bigger and better in the open market. He started adding olive trees, sunflowers, and wheat fields as major signatures for his paintings. He created an Oeuvre of his work sold and profited him a lot. He started a purposeful career with colors that made his art so bright.

His psychological torture led to his death, and his works resurrected his legacy. He came to be known as "a misunderstood genius in the public imagination." Gogh passed away on July 27, 1890.

Lessons learned

> We Should Appreciate Life With All The Beautiful Colours It Comes With.

> With Enough Drive And Passion, If You Set Your Mind On A Certain Goal, You Can Achieve It.

> Always Embrace The Unique Points In You And Hence, Embrace Your Individuality.

Jeff Bezos: Little Experiments Create A Big Change.

(The Founder CEO of the Amazon company. He is an American business tycoon, media proprietor, and investor)

Life Experiences

Jeff Bezos has shown a lot of interest in technology ever since he was young. For example, he manipulated an electric alarm to keep his young siblings away from his bedroom at one time.

Jeff started his first work at McDonald's as a short-order line cook during the breakfast shift in high school. After that, he started working to support his expenses.

While at the University of Florida, he attended the student science training program. He was so bright and got tremendous remarks. He was a high-scoring valedictorian, a National Merit Scholar, and a Silver knight Award winner in 1982.

He went to Princeton University and majored in engineering and computer science. After his graduation in 1986, he was offered jobs at Intel, Bell Labs, and Andersen Consulting, where he worked for a short while. After that, he worked at several companies gaining more skills from different levels in the web industry. Then he decided to pursue his career in the technology world.

Bezos established his online bookstore in 1993. The company grew immensely with time because of Bezos's hard work. The company is now expanded and is regarded as one of the top online companies globally and offers services online, including video and audio streaming, cloud computing, and artificial intelligence, and has opened an Amazon Web Services.

In 1999, Amazon bought a 50 percent stake in Pets.com, but it lasted only a few years. He also founded Blue Origin, which deals with aerospace manufacturing and services of spaceflight.

In 2009, Amazon had to delete digital editions of two books from the Kindle devices of readers because the company did not have the proper rights for them. This put a cinch in the trust people had in them and thus incurred a massive loss of revenue

Instead of this loss, they launched the Amazon Fire Phone in 2014. However, this phone proved to be a flop because of superficial goals and improper planning.

Success

Bezos is a worldly giver to many organizations and supports college scholarships in his country. He has also contributed to climate change funds through Bezos Earth Fund.

Bezos has won a lot of recognition in his life and is termed the businessman of the year by Forbes. Elected to human space flight is also one of his outstanding achievements. In addition, he was once classified as the best-performing CEO of his time.

He appeared in Fortune's 50 best leaders three times, emerged the top once, and received a $250,000 prize for space commercialization.

Lessons learned

Be Open to Accepting All the Challenges Thrown On You.

Think as a Strategic, Progressive Thinker.

Hopefully these stories would inspire the readers to take some lessons and create their own impact for self and society.

Chapter 13

Success Blueprint for Entrepreneurs and Start Ups

"Remember to dream big, think long-term, achieve daily, and take baby steps. That is the key to long-term success."
- Robert Kiyosaki

Entrepreneurs, start ups, small businesses, and MSMEs are the backbone of any country for job creation and economic development. They are also the pathfinders during the journey to economic recovery, even during crisis times. Entrepreneurs spend much time, resources with passion in their start up ecosystem. In this chapter, key attributes are being discussed for how to avoid failures and wisdom thoughts for the success of entrepreneurs and start ups for their sustainable contributions in local and global economy.

Entrepreneurs take birth every day, struggle, fail, and die in their life cycle, and some survive and grow. Reasons and circumstances vary. We often say: only 1% of people search for success. This is because many of us are afraid of starting. When you love success, you try to work towards it. It is a golden spoon only after you have failed several times and accepted the failure as a part of a long journey towards success. Failure is not permanent. Failure is fundamental to growth. If we can learn from what went wrong and why we know what to avoid or alter in the future to avoid a repeat.

Why some entrepreneurs fail while others succeed?

No one starts a business expecting to fail. Starting an enterprise can be a lot of fun and excitement. Success requires a lot of planning and starting the business the right way. Entrepreneurship is easier if you start your business the right way. The worst part about a failing business is that the entrepreneur is unaware of it happening until it is often too late. It makes sense because if the entrepreneur really knew what he was doing wrong, he might have been able to save the business. Some entrepreneurs are in denial mode while others are unaware of their mistakes.

There are over millions and millions of small businesses globally. It's an impressive number. According to a Harvard Business School study the sad reality is that the *failure rate* of all U.S. enterprises after five years is over 50 percent, and over 70 percent after 10 years. The situation in other developing countries like India is also the same. There are often multiple explanations start-ups fail. It is a constant challenge. Businesses fail for many reasons.

Some of the most common reasons are:

No vision and Lack of focus and your own accountability and commitment

Leadership failure, poor management, wrong partnership lack of team spirit, lack of trust, poor communication and feedback mechanism, not focusing on core values

No differentiation and no uniqueness in product /service

Lack of short term and long-term right planning

Inappropriate location

Shortage of capital and other resources. Poor financial management and no eye on cash flow, funds diversion, sales resulting into lack of profit

Inadequate inventory management

Lack of understanding of customers and not focusing on customer's needs and involving them in product development

No appropriate marketing plans

Being over ambitious, over expansion and premature scaling

Not seeking guidance from Mentor(s)

Impact of Macroeconomic factors and turbulent times of crises and lack of strategic crisis management plan to deal with the "unexpected" like during corona pandemic and others

Inability to learn from failure with strong belief system with appropriate corrective mode

And many more and solution is to develop concise, actionable and measurable Successful Business Plan to increase your chances of success. Those that succeed are not the result of miracles. Entrepreneurs who lead businesses to success understand that it takes a carefully planned and executed strategy. A little luck also helps.

Success attributes for entrepreneurs and start ups.

The critical success attributes of a good entrepreneur or start-ups which distinguish it from others are:

Develop Self Empowering Mindset

Entrepreneurs must take good care of themselves: physically, emotionally, and spiritually to keep themselves in high esteem, focus on motivating and inspiring a team to meet the challenges.

Some practical tips:

> Believe in yourself with confidence and a positive mindset.
>
> Appreciate that you are capable, confident with positivity and energy.
>
> Stock up on fuel, emotional reserves, and coping mechanisms. Keep mind and body in fighting shape. Be calm and poised.
>
> Avoid negative people and thoughts.
>
> Develop a routine of self-care: a healthy diet, exercise, meditation, or whatever works best for you. Practice spiritual exercises as they fit your individual beliefs.
>
> Eat well, get enough sleep, exercise regularly, relaxation as meditation and deep breathing, spend time outdoors (six feet away from strangers),
>
> Connect with your partner, kids, or animals and virtually with friends and extended family,
>
> Seek more social support from work relationships, personal relationships, and friendships. Talk to people you trust
>
> Laugh, tell jokes, rent a comedy video; cry if you must; listen to soft music. Listen to loud music. Dance and sing to both.
>
> Attend a favorite activity or hobby.
>
> Write a short story or a poem.
>
> Draw a picture. • Light a candle. Light many candles. Read a favorite book or story.

Plan for at least two device-free periods of 30 minutes per day.

Write letters, cards, and notes to people to express your thoughts about the situation.

Write down what you think in your diary, impressions, and reactions.

Use positive self-talk. Avoid negative thoughts and negative talk Constantly think positive thoughts and that you can do it.

Be more conscious of managing your time and priorities; keep meetings short and brief. Avoid repetition.

Concentrate on only significant issues. Skip secondary tasks.

Focus on the more excellent vision you have of yourself, personally and professionally. Think about where you will be and what you will be doing a year from now.

Develop discipline and resilience in personal and professional life.

The above thoughts would develop your robust framework of mind with optimism and hope and create a collaborative **"can-do"** attitude.

Believe in self

Starting your business gives you freedom of ideas, which will drive you to your success only when you work on them. Just focus on fulfilling the highest expression of yourself. Have vision and a plan of where you want to reach. Be in the diverse seats of your own life otherwise; energy will drive you. Always do the right thing because this is what success entails. To every action, there is an equal and opposite reaction.

A college education is not always necessary. Most famous innovators and entrepreneurs never finished college. A common thread among many entrepreneurs is a dislike and frustration with formal education. They go there to get some information, and once they perceive all the limitations around it, they drop out and seek a better way. For example, Steve Jobs went to college to gain knowledge, not a degree. Steve Jobs hated the school/college. He was thinking creatively and wanted to do something new. Several talented individuals dropped out of school, including Henry Ford, Nicole Kidman, Bill Gates, Ralph Lauren, Walt Disney, Richard Branson, and Valentina Tereshkova, the first woman in space.

Mark Zuckerberg also felt the need to attend Harvard University for formal education, yet created the beginnings of Facebook as a hobby in his dorm room. This experience flourished into something bigger than anything a college degree might have offered. Similarly, several unknown geniuses in every country could never have an opportunity to develop a new idea due to a lack of resources or are borne into a class system that views them as inferior.

Here is an inspirational story of Sonam Wangchuk, an engineer, innovator, and education reformist from India :

His extraordinary life was the inspiration behind '3 Idiots', a viral Bollywood film. He was considered a stupid child in his early years due to his lack of responsiveness to his teachers and peers. But, later, he completed his education from Delhi and pursued B-Tech from NIT Srinagar. However, he had to finance his education due to the lack of consent of his father over his decision to study. He also completed two years of higher studies in Earthen Architecture from France.

During his graduation time, he founded the Students' Educational and Cultural Movement of Ladakh (SECMOL) in 1988 for the 'victims(children)' of an alien education system foisted on Ladakh. He also became the Founding Director of the revolutionary school, which admitted the kids written off as failures by society. Wangchuk's sole intent was to make learning fun and practical rather than subjecting kids to rote learning.

He came into popularity in 2009, when his story inspired Aamir Khan's character Phunsukh Wangdu or Rancho in the Rajkumar Hirani-directed film 3 Idiots. Later, his groundbreaking innovations like 'Ice Stupas' and solar heated mud huts put him on the global radar for finding sustainable solutions in challenging terrains.

Emotions and originality matter

Clarity of thought, purpose, belief, and future is needed. Do not shy away from "crazy" ideas that can make you foolish, thinking others expect them to deliver only stable, predictable results.

> *"Imagination is more important than knowledge."*
> *– Albert Einstein*

Learn from Tim Ferriss story

Tim Ferriss, the author of the best-selling book, *The 4-Hour Work Week*, was turned down by 25 publishers before finally striking a deal. On the surface, this looks like another story that we've all read a thousand times: *belief in yourself, and good things will happen.*

But in a recent episode on his podcast, "The Tim Ferriss Show," Tim shared about this experience:

"I think I would add to that informed perseverance. Because I believe that you can smash your head against a wall and never breakthrough, but if you have some informational advantage, meaning, in my case, I had this feedback from students. I knew that the material worked in front of live audiences, including people who would land squarely in the demography where the book would be sold.

So I do think that's a huge component. If you have informed belief, committing to persevere through the pain, I believe, is a significant deciding factor."

Informed perseverance. Not just *"I believed in myself"* or *"I just knew."* Instead, there was evidence. There was work on the front end that proved to Ferriss that he had something, and it was just a matter of time before a publisher would notice. Ferriss had a workshop with his ideas with students at a University that fit the profile of his ideal audience. It worked. He had results with evidence.

Ferriss wasn't just guessing and hoping it would work. Instead, he had real-life, measurable evidence that his work was valuable.

The 4-Hour Work Week (which is not about working 4 hours a week) has been translated into 40 languages, sold over 2.1 million copies, and has become one of the most influential books to this generation's best creators and entrepreneurs of the last decade-plus including many start-ups in Silicon Valley.

When we hear stories like these, our initial reaction is belief, hope, and confidence in ourselves with action.

Success is the game of timing and correct decisions

When you want more time to make a correct decision, remember: even a right decision is wrong when it's too late..! Therefore, Anticipate, Adjust, Accelerate. You have to anticipate that things may go wrong; you have to plan for things to go wrong. And then once they do, you have to adjust. Sometimes your goal stays the same, but the strategy or the plan to get to a goal changes. Everything comes to you at the right moment. Be patient.

There is a narration that an elephant and a dog became pregnant simultaneously. Three months down the line, the dog gave birth to six puppies. Six months later, the dog was pregnant again, and nine months on, it gave birth to another dozen puppies. The pattern continued.

The dog approached the elephant in the eighteenth month, questioning, "Are you sure you are pregnant? We became pregnant on the same date, I have given birth three times to a dozen puppies, and they are now grown to become big dogs, yet you are still pregnant. What's going on?

The elephant replied, "There is something I want you to understand. What I am carrying is not a puppy but an elephant. I only give birth to one in two years. When my baby hits the ground, the Earth feels it. When my baby crosses the road, human beings stop and watch in admiration. What I carry draws attention. So, what I'm carrying is mighty and great."

Therefore, don't lose faith and be envious of others' testimony. If you haven't received your blessings, don't despair. Instead, say to yourself, "My time is coming, and when it hits the earth's surface, people will admire."

Take a moment to pause and plan to face adversities

We always fight and struggle. Always take a moment to pause and study the situation. You may find that there is nothing to fight. There is a story of the River and the Lion from the book "The little book of Letting Go" by Hugh Prather:

"After the plentiful rains, the lion was trying to cross the river encircled him. Swimming was not his nature, but it was either cross or die.

The lion roared and charged the river earth's surface before he retreated. Many more times, he attacked the water, and each time he failed to cross.

Exhausted, the lion lay down, and in his quietness, he heard the river say, "Never fight what isn't here."

The lion looked up and asked, "What isn't here?"

"Your enemy isn't here," answered the river. "Just as you are a lion, I am merely a river."

Now the lion sat very still and studied the ways of the river. Then, after a while, he walked to where a certain current brushed against the shore and, stepping in, floated to the other side."

Remove extra lemon from water

An interesting story goes like this:

"I still remember the day I was preparing fresh lime water for the first time. I ended up adding almost five times the amount of lemon than needed. It was a disaster. I had to correct it anyhow.

I wish I could remove some lemon juice from the water to make it taste perfect again! But alas!

Some things can never be undone. Some items can never be changed. There was no way that I knew of removing the extra lime. So what was the solution then? The only way to correct this was to add four more glasses of water and dilute the lemon juice to make five glasses of fresh lime water.

Sometimes we cannot undo some things that have gone wrong in life. Bad decisions, wrong choices, inappropriate investments, wrong actions, wrong associations, wrong words, or wrongdoings can never be undone.

So the solution is:

When you cannot correct what is wrong, do not waste more time on it. It is like attempting to remove lemon from water. Instead, get busy adding the right things in your life that the wrong seems insignificant.

We all have a negative side to ourselves. We may not be able to remove or correct all our negativities. But we can definitely continue adding positive thoughts, positive reading, and positive people in our lives and dilute the negativity. We all have to deal with some easy people and some difficult people

Do not waste time trying to change negative people. You will drain all your emotional energy in vain. Instead, spending more time with the pleasant, positive, happy people and the difficult people will not affect you anymore.

"I need help" Isn't a Weakness: *just ask for it*

Asking for help isn't easy, but it is needed to seek directions. There are times in business and job when all of us need help. It could be as simple as a ride to the airport or some advice on handling certain situations in our careers. Many of us don't want to have to go there. It's a more empowering feeling to know that we managed it independently. Still, this doesn't change the fact that sometimes we need help. So, if there is something, anything, you need help with, just ask for directions; you're more likely to find your destination much sooner after you ask.

Asking for help from people in your enterprise world makes you a great entrepreneur. You manage people who run an enterprise. You work with people who run a life. Trust their experience. It will save your business. And it will grow you and your people.

Here is one beautiful incidence:

Two candidates applied for the job of manager. The recruiter asked them one final question:

'What would you do when you are a manager and the economy goes down?'

The first candidate thought for a moment.

He wanted to leave a firm and robust impression. He said: 'I cut the costs, and I will do anything to save the company!'

The second candidate looked at the recruiter. She thought about her home and why she wanted the job. She said: 'I do not know. I would ask for help. Ask my people to put their experience at work. Ask my customers how they would like to be serviced when the weather turns sour.

The recruiter smiled. He looked at both candidates and said: 'We are looking for builders, and we are looking for people who find opportunities in any situation.

They hired the second candidate.

Again, ask for help and guidance. It works well.

Convert adversities into opportunities

In the face of adversity, when you curse your destiny or blame your fate, remember that if you set your mind to making your dreams come true, there's nothing that can stop you. No matter how small your beginnings are, you have it within yourself to reach somewhere in life.

There is a story: Two mice fell into a large bucket full of milk up to the top. One of them immediately gave up and died. But the other one utilized that opportunity to skim the milk into butter and finally came out of the bucket. Thus, the choice is yours, as in, which category you want to fall in. You must be the second one to stand out. Failure makes a person stronger. Every time you face failure, you learn something new. So, pray to fall more often so that you discover new points about your capabilities.

Before one learns how to ride a bicycle, they fall several times and never decide to quit till they get to do it the correct way. They push themselves harder till they become the best at riding bicycles.

Just because you failed at something does not mean you are a failure. We must consider failure as our Teacher, not the Undertaker. Failure can cause delay but not defeat. It is a temporary detour, not a dead end. You are not a failure. You do things that fail or succeed. And failing is just a stepping stone to success. Thus, it is entirely possible to turn a failure into success. When we fail to get what we want, at that time, we must look up to the standards that we set for ourselves. Success consists of going from failure to failure without the loss of enthusiasm and momentum.

The Harry Potter book, one of the most successful book series of all time, would not exist without the perseverance of J K Rowling. She got 12 rejection letters before a publisher finally accepted her story. This kind of perseverance and the ability to get up after a failure defines your character.

Always have a thirst for knowledge and strategic learning

Under Satya Nadella, Microsoft has gone from a window-centric lumbering giant to a 700 billion market cap-tech company, which strategically embeds on Artificial Intelligence and Cloud Technology. After a decade of flags were gone under his predecessor, the company's share price was raised to an all-time high. This is so amazing to hear, but how did he do it? He changed the company's mindset from a strategic perspective to a dynamic learning culture where everyone is comfortable learning new things and open enough to make mistakes in the process.

Always do something that you enjoy and can perform well. If you judge a fish by its ability to climb a tree, it will live its whole life believing it is stupid. Hence, there will be frustrating and disappointing moments in every field, whichever profession you choose. But, your belief will make the ride smoother. Happiness is a combination of pleasure and purpose.

Work hard and figure out what you want to do in life. Then, keep enjoying the process of watching a sunrise or hanging out with your friends. We all have different aspirations of what we want in our careers and lives. The right way is to adopt a holistic approach in our lives toward our job, family, friends, and hobbies so that we try to lead a fulfilling and prosperous life in all aspects.

We all suffer one of two things: the pain of struggles and failures or the pain of regret for not moving ahead. And never giving up is the only way to become successful in your entrepreneurship.

Continuously EVOLVE yourself

"Once you find yourself in a ditch, stop digging"
- Warren Buffet

Be a disciple of the *'problem-to solution'* method of entrepreneurism based on building from the market opportunity rather than the product. *Take actions and move ahead:* Create a strategy and emergency or backup plan, and don't struggle with thought paralysis and over-thinking.

E- Expand your horizon.

V- Varied options to choose from

O- Obtainable goals

L- Logical acts and movement

V- Valorous attempts

E- Emphasize encouraging milestones

Break down goals into manageable tasks to make decision-making with a clear focus on long-term plans. Review these tasks on a daily, monthly, and yearly basis so that they can be adjusted as per need. Finally, utilize the right set of influencers to grow your business, marketability, credibility, and name recognition. *Creativity is the new productivity:* In the age of artificial intelligence and machine learning, just being more productive won't work. The future belongs to creative individuals, entrepreneurs, and start ups.

Other actionable attributes

Time management skills: Value your precious time, once gone will not come again.

Treat everyone with dignity and courtesy.

Putting your customers first: When creating and marketing your product, you should have a mindset where you keep your customer first. Yet, many new entrepreneurs are so concerned about making money that they forget the key to a sustainable business is having satisfied, loyal customers who will buy your product or go for your services over the long term.

Always remember the mission statement of Amazon, ***"We aim to be Earth's most customer-centric company. Our mission is to continually raise the bar of the customer experience by using the internet and technology to help consumers find, discover, and buy anything, and empower businesses and content creators to maximize their success."*** This is an appropriate example for having a customer-first approach, as it focuses on customer services.

Inform your customers about updates: constant communication with the client is essential to avoid missing the customer experience bar of interest.

Evaluate your revenue streams and bottom lines, minimizing costs and maximizing your impact where it is needed. Identify active hours when you are more productive, which suit your working mentality and work life. Do not follow the work culture as decided by our society's norms since, during this pandemic situation, a complete shift has been noted. Nowadays, working from home is a necessity or demand of the case, not the choice. A new concept of 'work away from home is now emerging. So, therefore, with changing times, more unique ideas of work culture are developing, and we have to adapt according to the current ecosystem. The main aim should be precise even if small changes in the work environment are to be done as per the situation.

Take more tea breaks or short breaks, and this way, you relax your mind and refocus on your work with a clearer approach. The solution to all your problems starts pouring in during a calm state of mind. It is said that *'the best things happen over a cup of tea.'* Therefore, a tea break is a great option for teammates too. Remember to live your life while working on your enterprise. Enjoy each day and each moment. Learn to run the business and not vice-versa. Do not let the company run you.

Use support network: Take advantage of all government relief /concessions/moratorium/tax rebates/ packages. Avail benefits of the digital economy and social mobility, thereby ensuring newer customers' involvement.

Ensure that you as leader has weekly 1-on-1 meetings with all your team member with positivity.

Leverage Data and make sure that your enterprise and your employees are cyber secure.

Learn From Our Sports Heroes

Tokyo Olympics, World cup, and other games and sports teach us various positive leadership, motivation, teamwork, communication, goal setting, strategy, stress management, and other management lessons useful for entrepreneurs and all others for day-to-day activities. Some of them are:

> Have Perseverance, commitment, determination, and Resilience: if you fail: try again and again with adaptability.
>
> Hope for determination despite all odds and the critics and overcome extraordinary personal challenges and crises.
>
> Your dreams are reachable, no matter your age. Keep moving forward. be hopeful with a positive mindset. Never give up.
>
> Excellence has no upper limit.
>
> The ultimate competition is with yourself.
>
> Today, don't fear the shadows of yesterday; because a new day is for you, it is all pleasant and friendly.
>
> Performing to your limit doesn't give you a place on the podium, stretching it will.
>
> The team is not defined by the most decisive player but by its bench strength (players not playing on the ground but are in the group)
>
> Winning or losing is a game of just a few fractions so being alert & alive is the key.
>
> No opportunity is lost; competitors will grab it.
>
> Ultimately what matters the most is 'the moment of truth,' how you play the game rather than how you prepared & who coached you; four years of effort can go down under with just one silly mistake.
>
> You can win a gold medal only when you have the competency to overpower the best in the game when he

is in the best of form. Therefore, it is foolish to plan tactics around the weaknesses of the competitors.

Potential is the ticket to the stadium, but only performance can take you to the podium.

The actual coaches are competitors; they show possibilities.

Winners climb podium. Everyone else is a loser; the loss margin or the rank among losers isn't essential.

Winning gives you a new mission; losing provides a new purpose.

Celebrate every moment of success:

Celebrate every success, no matter how big or small. So, it is or how negative or positive is the outcome. Goals are great, but never become so singularly focused on the result that you as entrepreneurs/start-ups forget why it was even started in the first place. Entrepreneurs/start-ups should enjoy this process. It is a rollercoaster journey. Always savour small wins.

Learn from several inspiring idols, not just one. Else you force yourself into becoming a clone rather than a unique multi-skilled individual able to deal with, and most of all, one who can create change (only illustrative). Inspiration is drawn from any source/person, locally to globally.

Be fast like Bolt.
Persistent like Tiger Woods.
Daring like Senna.
Adaptive like Federer.
Forgiving like Madiba.
Creative like Elon Musk.
Intuitive like Darwin.

Curious like Edison.
Intuitive like Branson.
Enduring like Federer.
Inspirational like Churchill.
Tender like Mother Theresa.

Commitment and loyalty to nation like Ratan Tata

Successful people don't fear failure but understand that learning and corrective actions from failures are necessary. Consistent hard work leads to success. Never underestimate your life. It is most precious. You never know what talents are hidden within you and what you have to offer to the world.

You will surely lead your business towards growth and success. Even after the corona pandemic, there is tremendous scope for new business opportunities in every sector of the economy globally. In Indian context, the policies of the government ,viz, Make in India , Local to Global and many more are driving the economy and supporting this eco system. 'Sabka Saath, Sabka Vikas, Sabka Vishwas and Sabka Prayaas (Cooperation, development, trust and effort put by all) initiative further supports for active involvement of entrepreneurs for new economy.

Chapter 14

Success Attributes for Leaders

"Success consists of going from failure to failure without loss of enthusiasm."
– Winston Churchill

Leadership in every field is crucial for the success of any organization; its approach, strategic plans, and execution can either lead to success or doom to failure. Leaders are responsible and accountable, both personally and professionally, in creating strong teams, families, and companies. In tough times, the responsibility of leading by example and making appropriate decisions that impact individuals, communities, and societies are of vital significance. Leadership is not about avoiding the spotlight on one's actions, but in demonstrating methods and tools to handle unprecedented times with grace and vision. It is about evolution as much as it is about resolution and resilience. Being a genuine leader is a constant evolution with grace and awareness for the success of any organization.

Critical Factors for The Success of a Leader

Goalsetting, Motivation, Time management, Effective Communication, Delegation, periodic review, etc., are common and critical traits of a leader. Even a good manager and a supervisor possesses these traits. However, these traits alone do not make a person a successful and an authentic leader. Some specific traits required for a successful and authentic leader can be shortlisted as follows:

Be Your Own Manager for Your Lifestyle

Leaders face pressures from business and hectic lifestyles, so it is essential for them to keep physically and mentally fit to avoid chronic ailments. Rules, codes, or procedures that a leader lives by can bring more success, joy, and happiness through creativity and better decision making. Developing your practices provide freedom in life, and discipline equals freedom.

Personal self-care is like a battery, and it takes effort to keep it charged. Sleep, exercise, diet, journaling, walk and positive/pragmatic thinking keeps it charged. To keep oneself charged, it is advisable to follow some of the following steps regularly:

Morning time is your own glory time, and every day is a brand-new day

Every morning, when you wake up, begin with gratitude and start with thanksgiving; be thankful for what you already have and see the miracles that come from this one simple act. Also, be grateful to Almighty for this beautiful day, view outside the window, look out into the world for the opportunities and challenges, and align thoughts and action to strategize and dedicate the rest of the day to execute them.

Next, challenge yourself to develop more ideas than you need for yourself so you can share and give your ideas to others. That is called fruitfulness and abundance—it means working on producing more than you need for yourself to begin blessing others, blessing your nation, and blessing your enterprise.

Avoid checking your mobile/phone for the first 30-45 minutes of the day: Get the most critical, mentally demanding tasks done in the morning. Leave other routine work like emails, paperwork, social media, etc. for later.

Get enough sleep - 7-8 hours: Going to bed fixes stress, anger, and bad moods at a very high rate. Sleep is a powerful drug. Know how much sleep you need to be productive and to be in an active and positive mind-set.

Keep yourself hydrated: Drink lots of water to keep yourself hydrated; water helps digestion, stabilizes the heartbeat, flushes bacteria from your bladder, protects organs and tissues, and provides many other benefits.

Do some exercise/ yoga / walk regularly: Regular exercise/ yoga, brisk walking in the surroundings of nature helps to energize and improve your mood. It enhances your productivity as it releases endorphins and dopamine. Park the car in the back of a parking lot. It's an opportunity to get a few more steps in each day.

Deep Breathing 4x2x6x2 Helps: Just take (inhale) a deep breath for four seconds, hold it for two seconds and breathe out (Exhale) for six seconds and hold for 2 seconds. Repeat this cycle as much as you can, as per your convenience. This sets a harmony in your body and your thoughts.

> *Meditate or sit in silence* each day for at least 10 minutes twice a day and observe your thoughts. Accept yourself as you are.
>
> **Extend a helping hand** as and when needed, build a social network, talk to people regularly, practice kindness and compassion.

You own the phone. The phone doesn't own you. Don't answer your phone in the middle of a face-to-face conversation unless it's urgent. If you need to answer the phone, leave the room if your conversation disrupts someone else's work, discussion, or leisure. Others don't want to be a part of your conversation.

There is no reason to check emails, WhatsApp, Twitter, etc. several times a day. But, if it's that important, they will call.

Set priorities with passion, and don't overstretch.

Think positive and be positive.

Learn to say 'No' as and when needed. Figure out your priorities and reject everything else.

Listen first, don't react; respond.

Take action fast. Most of the activities take less than 5 minutes.

Don't schedule out every minute of your day. That leads to a miserable life.

Don't' play blame games. Stop making excuses and complaining. Start doing.

Learn from people who are already successful.

Journal every day with some details of your daily activities, emotions, performance, and new ideas. This would eliminate your stress too.

Read a lot and listen to related content, which has a vital role in your success. Buy books as they have the best ROI.

Make plans for free time to reduce stress. Continue with your hobby, which relaxes you. Hanging out with friends, exercising, heading to the mountains /close to nature, or doing anything physical is better at combating time stress than passive leisure such as watching TV.

Dress well, present well with confidence.

Always have 2 or 3 options for shirts that don't need ironing, and that can go with any color pants. Then, if you find a brand of clothes you like, buy them over at a sale price.

Other than for formal business activities, dress comfortably without embarrassing your spouse. Dressing like a "grown-up" always is outdated and a rule made up by people who don't smile.

Spend zero time wondering what others think about you or something you said.

Treat yourself occasionally and volunteer for services that you like doing.

Even giving up a few hours to volunteer at a charitable house, elders/nursing homes, teaching young, needy students, tree plantation, environment care, etc., may make you happier. Multiple studies have found that people who volunteer their time are more comfortable, healthier, and live longer. In addition, giving away time boosts one's sense of personal competence and efficiency. Smile, laugh, and giggle with your kids — no matter how stressful your day was. It's not their responsibility to deal with it.

Tell your spouse and children you love them more often than you. Nobody ever hears this too much.

Value time. Time is more important than money, and it has a price attached to it. Money buys stuff. Time buys meaningful relationships.

Attract opportunities, knock down obstacles and realize your potential.

Explore the unique, endless possibilities within you. Remember that when you work on improving yourself, you're adding to your mind's youth, vitality, and beauty.

Add value to others. Days are simply a series of habits. Live your days practicing the patterns that represent who you want to be in the future. Observe your way of daily life and understand yourself.

Ensure Frequent SWOT (Strengths/ Weaknesses/ Opportunities/ Threats) Analysis of Yourself

Knowing yourself is the beginning of your success. The foundation of successful leadership is your character, including integrity, honesty, perseverance, self-confidence, positivity, capacity to accept challenges with courage, competence, authenticity, and trust.

Leaders with high self-awareness understand where they are heading and what motivates them. By knowing their strengths and weakness, values, and aspirations, and how they affect the actions of others, they are likely to be able to make better decisions and ultimately lead others in the organization.

All these traits would enable leaders to think out of the box, be creative and make bold decisions in any situation. especially during tough times.

Create A Positive, Sustainable Organizational Culture with a Sustainable Vision

As culture is foundational to organizational success, Leaders need to create and nurture positive, sustainable organizational culture aligned with business purpose and the core values which the organization wants to sustain and develop for success in the long run.

To inspire and empower others, leaders need to define and create a vision, communicate the purpose, create organizational clarity, and foster an environment that allows the team to find the best ways to achieve the objectives. The vision needs to be something that inspires the team with a common purpose. Also, *a leader needs to be flexible* to realign with changing times.

In the early 90s, entrepreneur and author John Elkington coined the term **'triple bottom line: People, Planet and Profit.** The visionary leaders who genuinely make a difference in their organizations, communities, and society don't just pick one end goal to focus on; they strive to create organizations that serve all **three Ps.**

Care for Employees and Community with Empathy and Agility

> *"The secret to success is good leadership, and good leadership is all about making the lives of your team members or workers better."*
> *-Tony Dungy, Former NFL Head Coach*

Satya Nadella, CEO of Microsoft, emphasizes that "I think of empathy, not as something nice to have but something core to our organizational plan.

Any organization, big or small, is made by its team members. So, a good leader needs to do all he can to ensure the wellness of his team members as well.

Leaders need to ensure a robust and resilient workforce for the future and must care profoundly and consistently about their people – their health, their needs, and even their fears. Ignoring the human side of challenging circumstances can leave employees disconnected and unmotivated. A leader cannot ignore the anxiety people feel ignoring only magnifies it.

Empathize with how your people think and feel. Bring it out into the open and make them feel safe through healthy communication. *It is said that one doesn't have to operate with great malice to do great harm. The absence of empathy and understanding is sufficient.*

A leader's job is to bring the facts about "exactly where we are" to their organization and teams. Uncertainty and ambiguity are harmful, particularly during times of crisis.

A good business leader is expected to be agile in thinking and actions and be empathetic. **Nobel laureate Maya Angelou says, *'I have learned that people will forget what you said, people will forget what you did, but people will never forget how you made them feel.'***

Build Trust and have Crystal Clear Cut Communication

"The one thing I have learned is: Don't lie to the people. Don't tell your people one thing when the reality is something different."
- Indra Nooyi, Former CEO, PepsiCo

A leader who only paints rosy pictures might sound pleasant to their ears. Still, stakeholders prefer a business leader who lays down the image exactly as it is, without any sweeteners. He would, of course, keep talking about the good things they have in their favor and the dreams that they all can see together. But he doesn't mince his words when it comes to caution them about difficulties that might lie ahead. Such an attitude helps in generating and building trust among all the stakeholders.

George Bernard Shaw said that *"The single biggest problem in communication is the illusion that it has taken place."*

Remember, besides internal communication, the external world of competitors, present and potential customers, political lobbies, the press, business commentators, and others need to know the realities of the organization in clear terms. Therefore, a leader must communicate with complete sensitivity of how the world would accept his words and what kind of an impact his words and actions might make.

Be A Successful Leader through Emotional Connection and Humility

The world is changing faster than ever before, it is facing emerging uncertainties and the impact of pandemic crises. All leaders must deal with significant trends, including climate change, digital transformation, cyber security, globalization, terrorist activities, cross-border cultural issues with resilience, open mind, and agile adaptability.

Some of the leadership traits of your experience might become barriers in the changing dynamic world. So, leaders need to unlearn some of the frameworks they have based on their expertise to face the changing situations with a pragmatic vision for the future with *new normal*.

With the changes in socio-economic factors and market dynamics, organizations need to transform their strategies to survive and grow. Old rules and strategies are to be rewritten. Leaders need to develop wisdom for developing new strategies for future success with total conviction, commitment, and aspirations without any personal bias.

Leaders are to show their ownership, lead from the front, and build expected momentum by investing in people through continuous dialog.

We've seen through the changes and challenges during 2021, and expect the new opportunities and possibilities, the better ways of performance in the corporate world. New jobs, new skills, talents, and new work cultures are emerging.

In a recent McKinsey report, they expect the economy to be growing, but with a very different mix of jobs. There would be declining demand for customer-service roles, food services, essential office work—administrative assistants, and production facilities. In the United States, there are about 17 million people in jobs that may see less demand. Over the eight countries they studied ,100 million people may need skills to perform different occupations in new emerging areas.

Vince Lombardi highlighted a long time ago, *"Leaders aren't born, they are made. And they are made just like anything else, through hard work".*

Strategize and Develop the Wisdom to Face the Crisis

"The Chinese use two brush strokes to write the word 'crisis.' One brush stroke stands for danger: the other for opportunity. In a crisis, be aware of the risk - but recognize the opportunity".
-John F. Kennedy

We all agree that human race has been facing natural or artificial crisis, which creates in us a fear of the unknown and uncertainty more than ever before. People have high expectations from corporate and political leaders. The leadership of the 21st century must draw lessons from the past and design a bright future. The administration is all about managing diverse forces in society or business competition to make life purposeful. Mother nature keeps us alive to perform our duties to live and let live.

Leadership is to become a self- example in society and motivate others. Leadership must identify more prominent leaders for guidance and motivation that lead to self-actualization. To face these challenges and emergencies, focus on core strengths of self, family, community, and the nation to be a part of the global management system. We need to re-look at unit, human, family, and organizational values under a given political system and synergize society towards an action-oriented force at the national or international level to face such challenges.

The leader must have a core strategic team in place during a crisis. Such a team would ideally have members with different expertise and from multiple levels in the hierarchy. This team would be the sounding board for the leader to take their opinion about his broad strategy and specific ideas. This team would also be tasked with achieving buy-ins from the rest of the employees regarding the overall strategy and direction.

Last but not least, prompt firefighting of immediate problems would be the primary responsibility of such a team, instead of laying down the long-term strategy. But the team must remember that the solutions they provide should be descended to the organization's core mission with a realignment of priorities.

Remember the message of Peter Drucker: "The greatest danger of turbulence is not the turbulence; it is to act with yesterday's logic."

There is a story that seems appropriate to share:

A little girl is on a flight, and there is a lot of turbulence. She sits bravely while the rest of the passengers are terrified. When asked why she wasn't scared, she answered, **"My dad is the pilot, and he is taking me home."**

Remember the statement of Azim Premji, Founder Chairman of WIPRO; "The significant measure of leaders is not where they stand in the moments of comfort, but where they stand at times of challenges and crisis."

As a natural, authentic leader, you would never run away from a challenge because you are afraid. Instead, you would run towards it because the only way is to face it confidently and boldly.

Lead People for Success

Make genuine efforts to understand your team, facilitate positive feedback mechanisms, and seek creative solutions to the problems.

Accept that we all have flaws. No one is perfect. Accept others for who they are with grace instead of trying to fix their weaknesses. No one on your team should feel like they can't contribute because they're worried about being wrong. Instead, leaders who lead with love empower people to act authentically.

Be brave enough to have tough, vulnerable conversations. Being brave enough to have tough, vulnerable conversations is about giving constructive feedback from a place of understanding the situation or any challenges being faced — and working to reach solutions together.

Approach everything from a caring standpoint. Leading with love in the workplace doesn't mean you can't be upfront with people or that you have to let constructive feedback fall by the wayside. You can continue to create a safe space while remaining in charge of your company, squad, or department.

Show appreciation without expecting anything in return. Workers enjoy a higher success rate when their leaders show gratitude. This makes perfect sense: If leaders reward (verbally or financially) for the good things that staff members do, they'll do it again. Additionally, other team players will also emulate the practice.

Be a coach/mentor, not a critic. Coaching/mentoring will produce more innovation, and innovation is what your business needs to remain competitive in the economy.

Mentorship has another positive side effect-the most talented superstars in your organization will embrace leading with love in the workplace as they embark on their professional journeys for years to come.

A recent McKinsey & Company research finding revealed four times the job engagement among workers whose organizations have shown support, and have been pragmatic even in pandemic time. With emotional connection with employees and society, the leaders and their organizations succeed and make a difference.

Develop collaborative environment with humility and lead from the front Great businesspeople, Bill Gates, Richard Branson, Ratan Tata, Steve Jobs, Elon Musk, and others are visionaries and humble leaders. Humility enables leaders to form a team where every team member can give their high-performance outcome and work in a collaborative environment with mutual respect and happiness. And in the present context, it is crucial to keep the new generations of employees constantly motivated, inspired, and performing at their best, not with authority but through leading from the front.

Leadership is Challenging but it is Beautiful

"The challenge of leadership is to be strong, but not rude; be kind, but not weak; be bold, but not bully; be thoughtful, but not lazy; be humble, but not timid; be proud, but not arrogant."
— Jim Rohn, Author, Entrepreneur, and Motivational Speaker

To excel and be a successful leader, you need to be proactive and demonstrate your leadership in defining, leading and driving the activities beyond your regular duties. The above inputs would enable you to show your leadership in any situation.

Still, the best thing to do is to force yourself to stretch your capability, learn new skills, establish your credibility by emotionally connecting to all stakeholders with authenticity and a caring attitude and compliance of social and regulatory requirements.

Chapter 15

Ultimately Life is for Happiness

Success is a journey. Not the destination. ***Happiness Matters.***

Lord Krishna's advice: Everything comes and goes in life:
(Bhagavad Gita Chapter 2:47)

Our life is a long journey with a mix of struggles, failures, and success at every moment. Every time it is not successful as per our expectations, we must struggle and survive every day to get the best results for our desired success. Every day we must start the day with prayer immediately after getting up from our bed and say thanks to God for giving us one more opportunity to survive and be successful in this world. Start your day with a smile. Be happy and enjoy yourself. Love yourself. Love your work. Start the day with a new mood. Just do it differently than yesterday and try to improve something new and create happiness. You will undoubtedly get the chance to perform to the best of your ability. Just because you failed at something does not mean you are a failure and cannot create new opportunities. In every doubt, confusion, or struggle, take the higher path – the path of compassion, courage, understanding, and love. Happiness is not something readymade, it comes from our actions.

Life is a fingerprint that cannot be duplicated. So, make the best impression with it—Live it., Love it, and don't waste a single moment in your life. Because time has no holiday, Dreams have no expiry date, and life has no pause button!

Life isn't always comprised of Happiness. It is just an emotion that is the result of a situation based on feeling and contentment. Happiness is not a reward for escaping pain, instead, it demands that you confront negative emotions head-on; this creates the understanding that the term happiness is temporary within an individual until another emotional state overrides it. Happiness is not about eliminating bad moods or smiling all the time. However, it is about the depth of your feelings.

Be strong physically and mentally; things would get done faster, better, and more accessible. Among other things, make it a habit to recharge yourself with activities that relax you and boost your energy. Finally, do the things that make you happy! Happiness is a combination of pleasure and purpose. Find out the sense of purpose in your job, career, entrepreneurship, business, and life.

For Happiness in life, develop an attitude of gratitude by being positive in life rather than murmuring on the negatives. Various research studies have shown that appreciation touches on many aspects of our lives like our personality, emotions, social dynamics, career success, and health.

Gratitude strengthens our positive self-esteem emotions. Develops our personality and boosts our recognition in friends and society. Gratitude makes us more optimistic, and we feel better and happy about ourselves with good health, more energetic, and a positive mind. With our current life comfortable and sound, we will also believe in our future to have more significant potential for good and happiness. It is the single most powerful method of increasing Happiness and does not cost money.

Gratitude makes you a more effective manager by increasing your decision making, productivity, networking, and your decision-making capabilities, productivity, and in turn to achieve your career goals. It also makes your workplace a more friendly and enjoyable place. Gratitude changes your life.

Happiness is determined by its consequences and context; an individual can remain happy for an extended amount of time, or until the context changes and requires another emotion. Happiness derives from an individual's ability to be optimistic about consequences and behaviour. The inability to focus and achieve the set goals is a failure. Aspects of everyday life include family, relatives, colleagues, and networks of friends. These relationships create happiness through shared memories, experiences, and empathy. Relationships require emotional connection as relationship failure can result in conflict and detachment.

Another significant aspect of Happiness in life is leisure and recreational activities; these activities build personality and initiate freedom. Moreover, leisure activities maintain happiness and inner equilibrium as they are selected by each individual. Therefore, to be happy and to improve your life, focus on your hobbies regularly.

Richard Branson, an English business tycoon and philanthropist who owns the Virgin Group said that "a person can attract any happiness in the world just by being happy and find happiness in small and little things. Enjoy every day of your life. Define your own instead of copying other people's paths. Acquiring skills and talent is equally and more important than just acquiring formal education." The world is an oyster for you, and you can lead in any way you wish. Therefore, manage and balance your own life: professional, personal, family, and social for Happiness. Also, have a physically strong body enough to keep you active and strong emotional connect with society, Nature, and the planet. Have fun in your life and try to help those less fortunate. Have a whole heart of love, care, compassion, empathy, and concern towards surroundings. Finally, our divine destination of soulful life is to do some religious act that will lift society or the globe at large.

Remember the words of Ratan Tata, Chairman Emeritus of Tata Group: "No success or achievement in material terms is worthwhile unless it serves the needs and interests of the country and its people and is achieved by fair and honest means."

Life is precious and sacred. Life is a bundle of secrets, mysteries, and blessings. If we respect life, life respects us. The Covid 19 pandemic has unleashed sadness, misery, death, destruction on millions, and the only way for our survival is by staying together, being compassionate, and helping each other as much as we can. Besides Covid 19, another developments of Taliban & Afghanistan and Russia & Ukraine incidences have given us big lessons that nothing belongs to us, even our life.

Every struggle, adversity, failure, defeat, heartbreak, and loss contain its seed, its own lesson on how to improve your performance the next time. We can develop courage by being happy every day. We create it by surviving difficult times and challenging adversity. Life's challenges are not supposed to paralyze you; they're supposed to help you discover who you are. And once the storm is over, you won't remember how you made it through, how you managed to survive. You won't even be sure whether the storm is over. But one thing is sure. When you come out of the shower, you won't be the same person who walked in. That's what this storm's all about.

Life is a Game of Five Balls

Google CEO Sundar Pichai, in his speech for only 60 seconds, said:

Imagine life is a game of 5 balls that you manipulate in the air trying not to fall these balls. One of them is rubber, and the rest is glass. These five balls are work, family, health, friends, soul.

It will not be long before you realize that (work) is a rubber ball. Whenever you fall, you will jump again, while the other balls are made of glass. If one fails, it will not return to its previous form. It will either be damaged, bruised, cracked, or even scattered.

You must be aware of that and strive for it. Manage your work efficiently during working hours, take the time to be assured of your sincerity, give the necessary time to your family and friends, take appropriate rest, and take care of your health. It isn't easy to return if you are gone as, it was.

Let's follow Lord Krishna's advice: "Everything comes and goes in life. Happiness and unhappiness are temporary experiences that arise from sense perception. Likewise, heat and cold, pleasure and pain will come and go. They are never last forever. So, do not get attached to them. You only have the right to act (Karma)."

We would conclude this book by mentioning a very heart-warming and wonderful story, entitled:

Try to Touch the Lives of Others:

"I want to remember your face so that when I meet you in heaven, I will be able to recognize you and thank you once again."*

When Nigerian billionaire Femi Otedola in a telephone interview, was asked by the radio presenter, "Sir, what can you remember made you the happiest man in life?"

"I have gone through four stages of happiness in life, and finally, I understood the meaning of true happiness."
-Femi

In his own narration:

The first stage was to accumulate wealth and means. But at this stage I did not get the happiness I wanted.

Then came the second stage of collecting valuables and items. But I realized that the effect of this thing is also temporary, and the lustre of valuable things does not last long.

Then came the third stage of getting big projects. That was when I held 95% of the diesel supply in Nigeria and Africa. I was also the largest vessel owner in Africa and Asia. But even here, I did not get the happiness I had imagined.

The fourth stage was when a friend of mine asked me to buy a wheelchair for some disabled children. Just about 200 kids.

At the friend's request, I immediately bought the wheelchairs.

But the friend insisted that I go with him and hand over the wheelchairs to the children. So, I got ready and went with him.

There I gave these wheelchairs to these children with my own hands. I saw the strange glow of Happiness on the faces of these children. I saw them all sitting on wheelchairs, moving around, and having fun.

It was as if they had arrived at a picnic spot where they were sharing a jackpot winning.

I felt REAL joy inside me. Then, when I decided to leave, one of the kids grabbed my legs. I tried to free my legs gently, but the child stared at my face and held my legs tightly.

I bent down and asked the child: Do you need something else?

The answer this child gave me made me happy and changed my attitude to life completely. This child said:

"I want to remember your face so that when I meet you in heaven, I will be able to recognize you and thank you once again."

What would you be remembered for after you leave that office or place?

Will anyone desire to see your face again where it all matters? We pray to the Almighty that it does the same to everyone.

Tomorrow is another day of happiness and success. So, ultimately "Success is a journey...not a Destination!!!!" Appreciate, create, and spread happiness with solid emotional resilience, bondage, and values.

End Note: Keep On Walking

Neha Sharma

They might try to clip your wings …
They might try to mock your pains…
They might try to poke your wounds...
They might try to emulate your deeds...
They might try to ruin your happiness...
They might try to sabotage your manoeuvres...

But you keep on walking the path you think is right...
And shine as the glaring Sun… scintillating and bright...

They might try to rob your smile...
They might try to criticize your ways...
They might try to counter your thinking...
They might try to throttle your courage...
They might try to contain your passions...
They might try to test your resilience...
But you keep on doing good, with all your wit and courage.
And let your divine fragrance spread around aromatic galore.

Happy reading.

…………………..

Acknowledgements

My beloved wife Rama for her immense love, motivation, and encouragement.

My lovely daughter Dr Rachna, son in law Dr Pankaj and grands: Ishaa & Riyaa for their affectionate support and care.

My co-author Neha Sharma who has contributed with her beautiful thoughts and expressions in the chapters with her passion and dedication.

All those who have taught me lessons in my personal, social and professional life that infused courage in me to come out with positivity.

All those leaders whose mention has been made in the book based on their published material.

Dr Krishna Sharma, Head ,English Dept. SKIT , Jaipur for her copy editing of Part 2 and Ms. Nandini Goyal for collection and compilations of success stories covered in Chapter 12.

Bluerose Publications Team for timely publication of the book with professionalism.

Finally, all those who created happy moments in my life.

&

All those who would learn some practical tips out of this book for leading themselves and their organizations in crises with empathy and care for people and society.

S P Garg

Acknowledgements

Inspiration, dedication, and commitment are the most important principles one can follow in the journey of life and success shall follow.

I express my sincere thanks to Prof S P Garg, for encouraging me to level-up my creativity and imagination through this endeavor. His guidance has been phenomenal.

I am also immensely obliged to my friends and family members for their constant support and motivation.

My life has been my teacher, my philosopher, and my guide. Whatever I have shared in the book, is what I have learnt throughout.

And most importantly, the support and love of my lifeline, my kids. Without their affection, warmth, and support, I won't be here.

Neha Sharma

Author's Profile: Prof. S P Garg

Prof. S P Garg is visiting Management Professor, Key Speaker, Mentor, Independent Consultant, Career Coach and Author with more than forty five years of multi-dimensional/ multi-functional managerial & professional experience of management of institutions, board functions, organizational development, HRM & Training, international business, banking operations, business development, strategic transformation including overseas assignments and academics/teaching (MBA Education). Prof Garg has special interest in Strategy Management, Transformation, Change Management, Leadership Development.

Prof. Garg is presently associated as Chief Patron & Chairman of Aask Education (Higher Education Consultancy organization), Executive Director, Jagan Institute of Management Studies (JIMS) Jaipur and Management Consultant to several startups. Prior, Prof Garg has been Dean, Management Studies at SKIT Jaipur (2014-17) and Professor and Chairperson, MDP, Training and Consultancy with Jaipuria Institute of Management , Jaipur (2009 -14).

Prof. Garg, 73, Jaipur born, is an Alumnus of IIM Ahmadabad (1973) with specialization in Agri Business Management besides Postgraduate in Agri Sciences from Pant Nagar University. He is also Certified Associate of Indian Institute of Bankers (CAIIB) and anagement (I).

During his corporate journey, Prof. Garg has been at various coveted positions viz. Dy General Manager Bank of Baroda,

Managing Director, BOBCARDS, Chief Executive, Fiji Operations, AGM, USA, New York Operations, Regional Manager, Chief Faculty, BOB Regional Rural Banks Staff College, Chairman of Sultanpur RRB and many more.

Prof. Garg has been actively associated with academic activities as Key Speaker / Resource Person for various Training Programs/ Seminars/ Symposium organized by various organizations/ Institutions/B-Schools and contributed as member to various Committees, Task-Forces set up by the RBI, NABARD, State Government & other institutions/ Organizations. He has been actively associated with HRM activities at corporate level in man power selection, training and development, talent management and career progression of young generation, Entrepreneurs and Startups with flair in Hindi.

Prof. Garg has active interest in institution & brand building, leadership development and mentoring; Corporate Social Responsibilities (CSR). He Loves nature and strongly believes in creating and spreading happiness across society. His earlier published two books "Anandmay Safal Jeevan" (in Hindi) and "Visionary Leadership in Crisis" have been loved and appreciated by the cross section of readers. Besides this book "Life and Success: the Ultimate Blueprint", one more book "APKE KADAM SAFALTA KI AUR" [in Hindi) would also be with readers shortly.

Mr. Garg has travelled very extensively to various counties: USA, UK, France, Australia, New Zealand, Singapore, Thailand, Fiji, Puerto Rico and others.

Presently, Prof. Garg is settled in Greater CHICAGO Area, US.

Contact: spgarg33@yahoo.co.in   www.spgarg.org

India: +91 9309292080 WhatsApp: USA: +1 708 800 6580

Author's Profile: Neha Sharma

Neha Sharma is an educator based in Mumbai, who has been working in this field for more than 10 years now. She started as a teacher, and marked her way towards the position of the Center Head. With constant and dedicated efforts, she is climbing the ladder of growth, step by step.

Always having had a flair for writing poetry and prose, she started penning down her thoughts and feelings in the form of soulful poems. Her poetry book which goes by the name," With Love" got published recently and was well appreciated by lovers of English poetry.

Neha started working as a freelance content writer and her website "nehazworld29.wixsite.com" is currently a thriving platform. By writing web content as well as articles and blogs for various organizations and individuals, she has been able to showcase her writing prowess.

After completing her graduation in humanities, she completed her master's in English Literature. Always mesmerized by the writings of some of the greatest names in the writing arena like William Shakespeare, Jane Austen, Robert Frost and many others, she was always drawn towards the concept of writing. She is perpetually trying to assimilate the depth of emotions and how their usage can help render a soul to mere words.

She believes in constant learning as once the learning stream stops flowing, life becomes stagnated.

Notes

www.ingramcontent.com/pod-product-compliance
Ingram Content Group UK Ltd.
Pitfield, Milton Keynes, MK11 3LW, UK
UKHW042003230426
12048UKWH00009B/526